NORFOLK
CHURCHES

NORFOLK CHURCHES

David Stanford

To my dear friend Richard Dyball,
whose support and enthusiasm for these books has been constant.

Frances Lincoln Ltd
4 Torriano Mews
Torriano Avenue
London NW5 2RZ
www.franceslincoln.com

Norfolk Churches

First Frances Lincoln edition 2007

A catalogue record for this book is available from the British Library.

ISBN: 978-0-7112-2742-2

Printed and bound in Singapore.

9 8 7 6 5 4 3 2 1

Frontispiece:
Copy to come
More details

CONTENTS

INTRODUCTION

Norfolk Churches is the third in this series, the first being *Suffolk Churches*, followed by *Essex Churches*. As with the previous titles all the photographs in this book were taken digitally on lower-end digital cameras rather than very expensive professional cameras, which to those not interested in photography will be unimportant, but to me it was a singular condition of my undertaking this project in the first place. I must therefore commend Frances Lincoln for allowing me free rein in my conviction that this was a realistic and professional way to proceed. I have completed professional assignments in places as diverse as Ethiopia, Peru, Australia and France, all with a variety of digital cameras and must admit that in the early days I cautiously covered everything on film as a kind of insurance policy, but the digital results increasingly spoke for themselves and I have not used film for many years now. It is now 2007 and all things digital have moved on at an astonishing pace; digital photography no longer begs a place at the table of serious creative photography. Yet still the governing maxim, applies: that nothing will make a bad picture good, no matter what equipment, methods or techniques are used.

That one of series would definitely be on Norfolk Churches was never in question but I decided to approach the project in the order it appeared partly due to travel logistics but also because I was less familiar with that county than the other two and needed time to find my feet. Essex had a obvious significance for me because, after arriving in the United Kingdom from Australia (at a time when most people were going the other way), I spent a part of my early life and teenage years living in that county, eventually studying painting at that Mecca of 1960s Art schools, Walthamstow, which during an all-too-short but glorious period turned out the likes of Ian Dury, Uncle Vivian Stanshall, Bill Jacklin and Peter Greenaway, to name but a few. I had an interest in history from my earliest years but, arriving in the UK to find it peppered with churches that represented living history, I was captured for life. Eventually I went to the Royal College of Art, and made frequent weekend forays to the countryside visiting Norfolk a number of times on painting expeditions which always (since I was the only one with a car I got to plan routes) managed to include, often to the surprise of my traveling companions, a few churches. Finally switching from painting I became absorbed in my new career as a fashion photographer and director of commercials and for many years this kept me too busy traveling the world on assignments to be able to indulge any other interests. After twenty-five years of this I decided to give up my studio in central London and the frenetic life I led to seek a slower pace in Sussex, cherry-picking only those assignments I chose to, and it was then I rediscovered old churches.

All of England's churches bear witness to their importance in history. These wonderful buildings offer a wealth of art and anecdote, often presented with age-old passion, and to miss them is to miss a compendium of uniquely moving experiences, spiritual and temporal. The sheer wealth of famously beautiful churches in Norfolk made selection just a little bit more complicated than Suffolk or Essex and the remoteness and isolation of many of them made the experience of visiting a real adventure. This also meant that many were, understandably, not open and, sadly, too many had no keyholder's name supplied, which has led to some being excluded from my final selection. However, that said, I don't think I was ever disappointed with the exterior of any church I visited. Norfolk is a county that has always been a little difficult to get to and that fact that has added to its mystery. It is a county of massive contrasts: wild coastline, sweeping plains, marshlands and of course the unique Norfolk Broads . . . a church-crawlers paradise.

As with Suffolk and Essex, this book contains an eclectic and very personal selection, not presented as a learned critique, but simply as one man's view of some of the churches of Norfolk. If the book encourages others to seek out and visit any of the churches it presents then it will have served a purpose. For me, discovering and visiting these wonderful buildings continues to be a remarkable journey and, having now looked at and photographed many hundreds of churches in all three counties, I am amazed that I still find it hard to pass a lovely old church without wanting to take a peek.

Reasons for visiting churches range from religious conviction through mere curiosity to a simple a day out, but each individual visit can provoke and stimulate thought outside our day-to-day experience. There is a paramount need for us to cherish these remarkable buildings and make sure they continue in the role they have played for centuries, through good times and bad, refuges for belief, contemplation, peace, wonder and the retelling of the myriad stories of humanity. So to close on a note of pure optimism, one can do no better than acclaim the wonderful example set by organizations such as 'Friends of Friendless Churches' whose tireless work has already saved many beautiful buildings that would otherwise have been lost for ever.

David Stanford

KEY

Ashwellthorpe G5
Aylmerton G2
Bawburgh G4
Beeston Regis G1
Bessingham G2
Binham F2
Booton G3
Broome I5
Burgh St Peter J5
Burnham Overy E1
Carleton Rode G5
Cley-next-the-Sea F1
Cranwich D5
Crostwight I2
East Lexham E3
Edingthorpe H2
Fishley I4
Frenze G6
Gissing G6
Gunton H2
Haddiscoe I5
Hales I5
Hethel G4
Kings Lynn C3
Little Barningham G2
Little Snoring F2
Loddon I5
Melton Constable G2
Merton E5
Narborough D4
Newton E3
Oxborough D4
Oxnead H3
Potter Heigham I3
Ranworth I3
Rockland F5
Salle G3
Seething H5
Shelton H5
Shimpling G6
Sisland I5
South Acre E4
Stanford E5
Stow Bardolph C4
Stratton Strawlesss H3
Tattersett E2
Terrington St Clement C3
Thompson E5
Tilney All Saints C3
Tuttington H3
Walpole B3
Waterden E2
Weeting D5
West Somerton I3
West Walton B4
Wheatacre J5
Wiggenhall C4
Wymondham G4

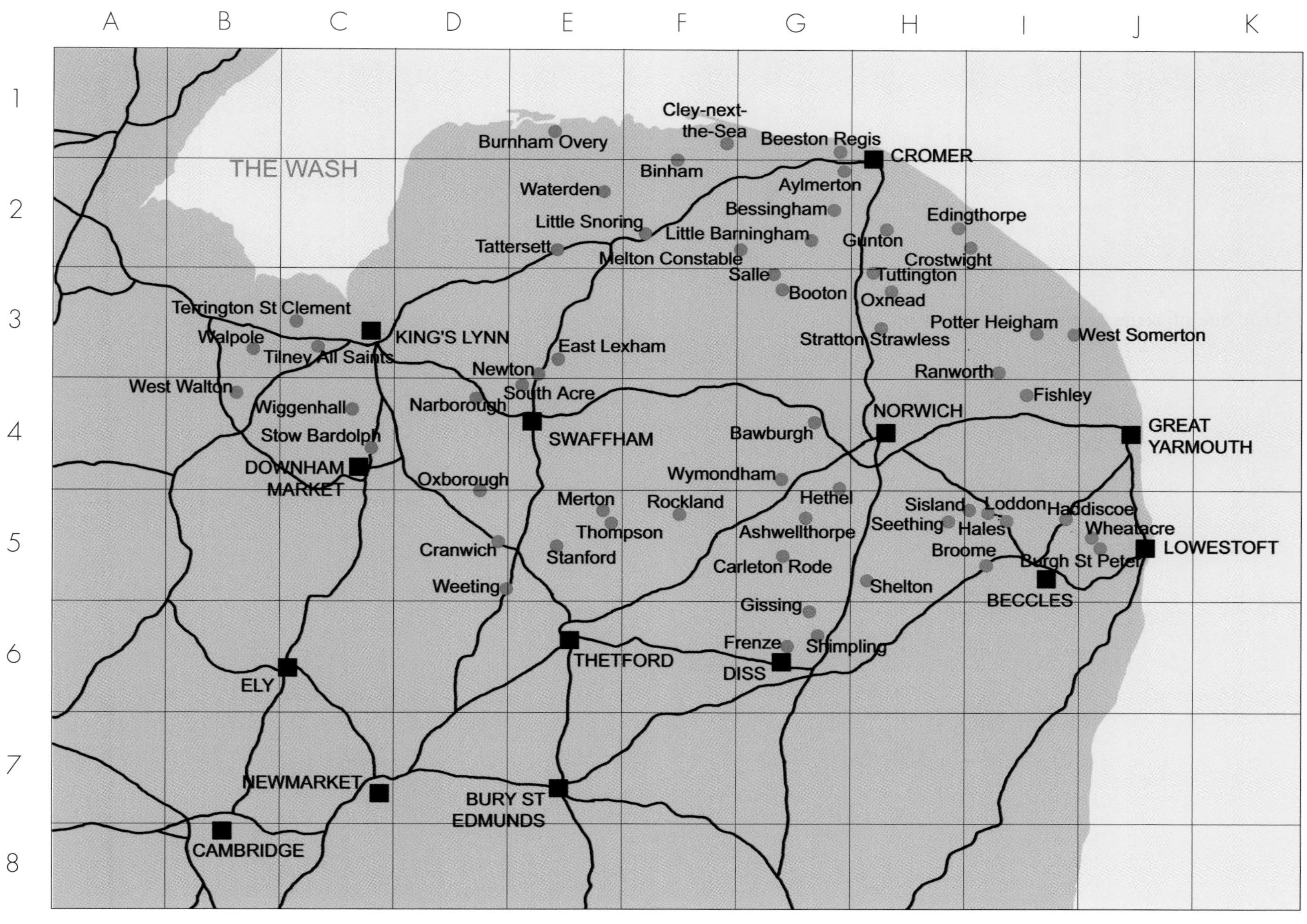

ALL SAINTS ASHWELLTHORPE

The alabaster tomb of Sir Edmund Thorp and his wife Joan

This building has lovely warm colouring. The square, heavily buttressed tower, is thirteenth century, topped with battlements and chequer work of a much later date. The addition of an eighteenth-century Dutch gable to the porch tends to disguise its Perpendicular origins and the chancel and nave are also Perpendicular, the nave being unusually tall in comparison to its length, an effect that is accentuated by its range of fifteenth-century windows.

However, the gem is the alabaster tomb of Sir Edmund Thorp and his wife Joan. After surviving Agincourt in 1415 Sir Edmund was killed at the siege of Louviers Castle in 1417, once again fighting under the command of Henry V. His body was brought back to England and buried here in the chapel he had built for himself and family. It is a superb piece. He lies in full armour, his heavily moustached head resting on an enormous, plumed war helm, an unsheathed dagger by his side and his wife next to him in fashionable gown and headdress. Angels lift her head up on a pillow while dogs play at their feet, and beneath them on each side of the tomb chest another angel bears the family arms. Most unusually they both wear the S collar of privilege.

Undoubtedly this is a very important historical artefact and the picture shown here has been heavily cropped since the monument is, at present, covered in scaffolding for essential restoration work. To my dismay, when I returned the key to a most obliging keyholder, he bemoaned the fact that the church was having to pay £4000 in VAT on top of the cost of the restoration, since the monument, the authorities claimed, is not part of the church and therefore not zero rated. Whichever way you look at it, this is a disgrace. How can such mindless unfairness be displayed towards such a national treasure and charged to a community that is struggling to raise the cost of the restoration? Anyway, since Sir Edmund died fighting for his country is this not, however ancient, a War Memorial? Surely they do not charge VAT on those. Perhaps the authorities should think again.

ST JOHN THE BAPTIST AYLMERTON

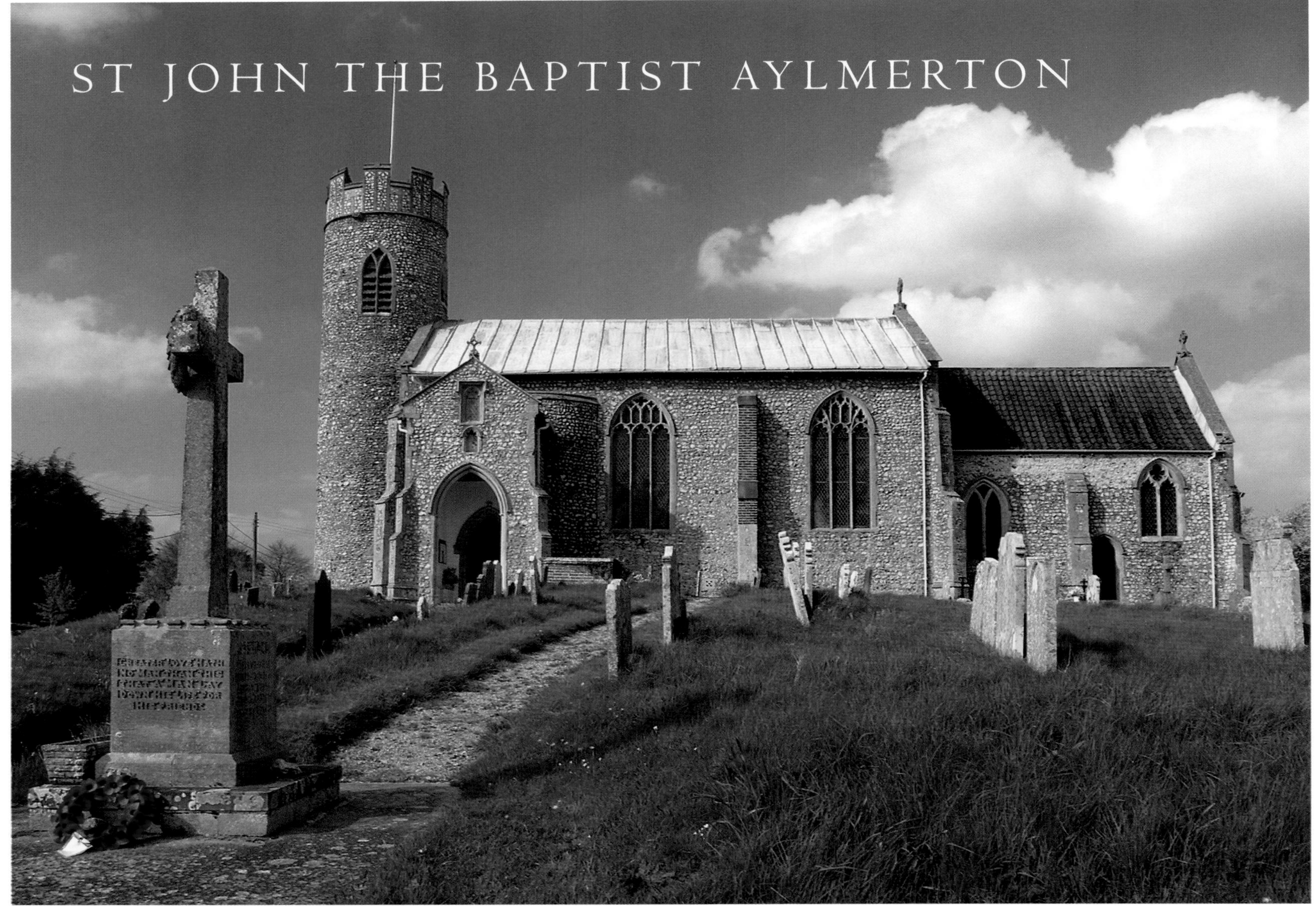

There may previously have been a Saxon timber building standing on this grassy slope but what we see now is a distinctly Norman round tower church. The building has seen many changes during its long history. The nave was added around 1200, further major alterations took place in *c.*1400, the chancel was rebuilt in the mid-fifteenth century, Victorian restorations took place in 1865 and again in 1876, and finally the upper part of the tower with its fifteenth-century battlements was restored in 1912.

In the fourteenth century John of Gaunt, the first Duke of Lancaster to be patron of this church, was a major landowner in this part of Norfolk. Through marriage he also became titular King of Castile, although he never governed it and after some seventeen years he resigned. Some similarities in decorative and heraldic devices around the building are thought by some to be a direct reference to this Castilian link but nothing has been conclusively proved on the matter.

The pleasant interior has a fragmentary screen with ogee arches and a pretty two-bay sedilia with a cusped and crocketted canopy and little round faces on the head stops. These heads can be seen again at the other end of the church by the holy water stoop, which was itself found lost behind a plastered wall in 1840.

ST MARY AND ST WALSTAN BAWBURGH

This extremely pretty little church, lying down a now quiet lane, gives little indication of the busy place it must have been in the Middle Ages. For this was the shrine of St Walstan, a local Norfolk saint, the patron saint of farm workers. It is known that St Walstan was buried here by the Bishop of Elmham in 1016 and, from then until the Reformation, many of the faithful would have travelled here for the healing powers attributed to the saint. With the coming of the Reformation, however, the bones of the saint were vindictively burnt and scattered under the auspices of the new religious beliefs and the local people were deprived of solace from one they must have considered as one of their own.

As always with round tower churches the question is: Saxon or Norman? In this case there can be little doubt this is a Saxon church, a fact borne out by the thickness of the walls of the tower, which gently slope inwards towards the top to be capped by a conical roof surmounted with an emblem representing the tongues of fire that come down to earth at Pentecost. Unexpectedly, the tower is not the oldest part of this church; this is in fact the west wall of the nave, on to which the tower was built. Records show that in 1309 the chancel was rebuilt with a splendid shrine chapel to the north of the nave but all that remains of this is an arch inside the church. Once its status as a shrine had gone, the church fell into disrepair. It was not until 1633 that it was renovated and made suitable for worship again. It was probably about this time that the charming and distinctive crow stepped red brick gables were added.

Just inside the door are the remains of a wall painting, which would have been limewashed over during the Reformation, and fragments of fifteenth-century glass have survived in the north and south windows. Little of the original screen exists but there are some bits of fifteenth-century oak incorporated into the present screen, which was completely rebuilt in 1905. A number of brasses are to be seen, including one of Robert Grote (1500), who was once accompanied by his wife, but she has long since disappeared. There are two shroud brasses, one for the vicar Thomas Tyard (1505) and the other Phillip Tenison (1660), the same year as the King Charles II arms that hang on the wall. Also to be seen, on a nearby farm is St Walstan's Well.

The nave and chancel

ALL SAINTS BEESTON REGIS

It takes a little imagination to see this spot as the lonely, dramatic place swept by sea spray that it must have been before the advent of the caravan sites and holiday bungalows that now flank it. From the sea, passing ships would have welcomed the sight of this church's soaring tower as a beacon; approached from the land it was a tidy stroll from any habitation in its earliest days. The location alone, high above the sea, begs closer investigation, with the massive unbuttressed square tower being first thing to come into view, its square proportions, so unlike most contemporary eleventh- or twelfth-century Norfolk churches, becoming more apparent as one gets closer. Then there is the clerestory, faced in square knapped flint. Its windows – and most of the others – are in the Perpendicular style, with the exception of the east window which alone is in the earlier Decorative style. The interior has a three-bay arcade, again in the earlier Decorative style, and a beautiful fifteenth-century rood screen. Although much restored after the ravages of time and religious bigotry, the screen's twelve panels depict, in the original colour, the apostles. More recently their names have been added to the much earlier paintings. The sedilia is odd in that it has been somewhat uncomfortably inserted into a window space. As one would expect this is a large airy interior with parts of the floors paved with black ledger-stones, some of which commemorate the Cremer family. Does the name relate to the nearby town of Cromer?

Rather quaintly, to get to the church in any vehicle higher than a normal car one has to stop at the level crossing and ring the station master from the telephone provided. He then instructs you to 'open the gate and cross quickly while all the time listening for oncoming trains'. On the way back the whole process is repeated, and all the while this massive building looks on in disbelief at modern progress.

ST MARY BESSINGHAM

The beauty of Norfolk's many round tower churches is often further enhanced by a wildly romantic setting and this lovely church, proudly standing on its ancient, perhaps man-made mound, bears witness to this. The classic outline of the tower confirms not only its Saxon origin but also identifies it as one of the earliest in the county, yet, unusually for such an early example, this tower is constructed not of flint but of carstone, known locally as gingerbread stone.

The nave and chancel, all under one roof, were rather uninspiringly restored in 1889, leaving an interior that can hardly compete with such an lovely exterior. Alas it was left containing little of interest other than a fifteenth-century pulpit and some stained glass by Kempe in a south side window. Nevertheless, the serene simplicity and strong line of the exterior, when coupled with this beautiful setting, is all that is needed to make this an extremely interesting little church.

ST MARY BINHAM

This Benedictine priory was founded in 1091 by Peter de Valoines, yet what remains owes its survival – and for that matter inclusion in this book – to the fact that it is also the parish church and always was. Its pedigree as a parish church is evidenced by an early seven-sacrament font, something that would never have been present in a purely monastic establishment. Essentially Norman in style, the church has the proportions of a cathedral and some might wonder why this would be in such a remote spot, but it becomes clear when it is remembered that Binham is on a direct route from the sea to Walsingham, one of the great medieval places of pilgrimage, so crowds of pilgrims would have passed through this place.

It is surrounded by the monastic buildings, now highly picturesque ruins thanks to Henry VIII. As a parish church Binham escaped the worst excesses of the Dissolution but nevertheless the superb west window was maliciously bricked up and the aisles, trancepts and all that smacked of the monastic was destroyed or allowed to decay and tumble.

The huge west window that received the Tudor brick treatment was the work of Prior Richard de Parco (1226–44) and with its use of bar tracery was the glory of the church. Bar tracery was an important French invention developed during the building of Reims Cathedral which was consecrated in 1241. This makes Binham the earliest use of the technique in England, predating similar work at Westminster Abbey.

Inside a towering interior the dado rails of the original screen now form the back support of the end row of pews. In Elizabethan times they were whitewashed over and the saints replaced by religious texts, but the saints are now making a comeback and as the whitewash fades they are remerging from beneath the text. There are also two badly damaged misericord chairs left over from monastic times and some excellent poppy headed bench ends carved with figures, but a little lion is the only one not to have been beheaded by religious bigots. The ironwork of the original rose window now hanging on the west wall of the interior gives a rarely seen glimpse of the skill of medieval builders.

Above: The west window
Left: The painted texts
Below: The bench ends

ST MICHAEL AND ALL SAINTS BOOTON

Some might question the inclusion of a church once described by the great Sir Edward Lutyens as 'very naughty but in the right spirit'; to leave it out, however, would be an injustice to the devotion and eccentricity of a country parson whose original wish to improve his crumbling parish church turned into a lifelong project of grandiose proportions. The Reverend Whitwell Elwin was its rector for fifty years, and without architectural experience or drawing ability of any kind he conceived the building, raised the finance and directed, sometimes incorrectly, the building works throughout its often problematic evolution. This interesting man was a descendant of the Native American princess Pocahontas, who came to England with her husband John Rolfe in 1617, was feted by James I, yet never saw her native Virginia again. She died of smallpox within a year and is buried at Gravesend. Although offered preferment, the reverend chose to remain a mere country parson, who numbered among his friends and acquaintances not only Dickens and Thackeray (who for some obscure reason called him Dr Primrose), but a host of other influential artists and politicians of the time. On top of all this the Reverend Elwin was something of a ladies man, admired for his conversation and striking, somewhat Native American good looks. He surrounded himself with a bevy of young ladies that he referred to as his 'Blessed Girls' and it was through them that a great deal of the finance for the building was raised.

Started around 1876 and finished about 1900, the church is built of knapped flint stone and according to Pevsner boasts 'an excess of pinnacles'. Such a view would not have worried the tireless vicar, who was able to indulge shamelessly his untutored fantasies in a way that no professional architect could ever have done, simply filching whatever style, accessory or detail from wherever it caught his eye on another building or illustration and the result of this cavalier approach is what we see today. All that remains of the original church are the walls of the nave and chancel. It is an indication of the hit-and-miss approach that, sadly, fairly early on in the building schedule the chancel started to sink into the family vault below and poor Elwin had the unpleasant task of reburying the decaying bodies of his ancestors elsewhere in the grounds before the underpinning, which should have been done beforehand, could be carried out. A surprisingly lofty interior exudes a Victorian coldness that the exterior hardly reflects, but there is still much to see, such as, high up on the hammerbeams, some marvellous carved angels by the master carver James Minns (1824–1904), whose carving of a bull's head is still featured on jars of Colmans mustard.

This is now one of many redundant churches but it remains open and welcoming and full of surprises.

ST MICHAEL BROOME

This is a special place for me. For some years, the Daishes, dear friends of mine, owned the seventeenth-century Dutch gabled mansion Broome Place, situated directly across the fields and woods from this church. I spent many memorable times as their guest, often making magical windswept walks to this very spot.

At first glance one might be forgiven for taking this to be a newer building than it actually is and one that might have little of interest, but that would be a great mistake. At the end of a lane, over a mile from its parish across an open field, it must always have taken considerable effort for the parishioners to reach it. Evidently it was not always completely isolated because Broome Hall (demolished in 1825) once stood next to it, but all trace has long since disappeared. This is a church that makes its main statement with its elegant west tower. It can be seen from far away, built in the Perpendicular style. It is pretty elaborate for a church of this size, the spandrels of its west door being heavily decorated with tracery and a plethora of shields. Above this door is a window with what Pevsner describes as 'dainty Perpendicular tracery' and above that a statue niche.

Inside, the wide nave the intricate tracery of the Perpendicular windows immediately captures the eye, and the chancel, also from about the same period, has the remains of a fine, stepped sedilia and an early-thirteenth-century priest's door. There are the remains of a two-figure brass of the de Broome family, inexplicably positioned in a window embrasure, where it appears to have been for a very long time. There are a number of hatchments of the Fowle family and another, the oldest, is that of Sir William Cooke (d.1681). The memorial wall tablet of Sir John Fowle (d.1731) has an exceedingly long Latin epitaph set upon a confection of crossed trumpets, wreaths and scrolls, watched over by two large putti hovering aloft.

Despite the distance from its congregation, this is a well cared for and obviously much loved church and it stands as evidence that often a closer look at the most unlikely buildings seen from afar will reveal much of the unexpected.

ST MARY BURGH ST PETER

The nave

Even the locals seem a little confused by this odd dedication which, for some unknowable reason, was changed from St Peter – from which the village name is derived – to St Mary in around 1764. As if that were not enough there was also a chapel 100 yards to the west which seems to have been dedicated to St John, but all trace of that has now disappeared. Further confusion lies in the fact that this church is nearly one and half winding miles away from its village and many local people can give no idea how to get there, so thank the lord for satnav.

Standing by the river Waveney, the building, which has been variously described as 'pagoda-like', 'a pyramid' and 'a monstrosity', is for me a simply a wonderful example of that great but dying English characteristic: eccentricity, and the effort of getting there is well worth while.

The west tower appears out of nowhere – a set of diminishing red brick boxes one upon the other, looking as though they would neatly telescope into one another like some sort of geometric brick Babushka. It is most aptly described by Pevsner as 'someone's folly' and it must be unique in England. The broad base of the tower with its diaper of flint is the earliest part and probably dates from the early sixteenth century, the upper four steps being added in 1793 by the rector Samuel Boycott. Yet, unexpectedly, apart from the eccentric tower this is in essence a thirteenth-century church. The nave and chancel are all one under a reed thatched roof and the earliest features are the north and south doorways which date from around 1200. Enter through the very snug little porch and under a fifteenth-century arch braced roof you will find a pleasant early-fifteenth-century octagonal font, an Early English mass dial as well as a fourteenth-century sedilia and piscina. The pulpit dating from 1811 carries a number of plaques pinpointing exactly where each of the Boycott family lies buried in brick vaults within the sealed off base storey of the tower, converted into a tomb for that family, rectors here for over 135 years. This lower section was originally the vestry but in adopting it as the Boycott family crypt the vestry was moved up a floor and is now approached through a narrow door and staircase.

The Boycotts not only gave us this extraordinary building but also a new word in the English dictionary. for which we can thank Charles Cunningham Boycott, second son of William Boycott, rector of this church in the nineteenth century. As a second son Charles could not inherit the living and therefore spent many years in Ireland farming. When the troubles came he was driven out by the locals who withdrew their services and sent him to Coventry, a position that became known as being boycotted.

ST CLEMENT BURNHAM OVERY

In a churchyard that has a number of graves of sea captains dating from the time that this was a busy port, it is easy to picture the young Horatio Nelson walking here, as he often did on his way to and from his home at the rectory at Burnham Thorpe.

With regard to this church, however, one can hardly do better than start with a quote from Mortlock. 'This is a church whose history and fabric raise enough questions and intriguing puzzlements to make one dizzy.' Virtually everything about this beguiling building prompts a question. It stands above a village that, although sheltered from the sea, is set high enough to merit not one, but two windmills in close proximity. St Clement is now significantly smaller than the altogether grander original building, which had both aisles and trancepts. Pevsner ponders whether there ever was a north aisle but the church has a cruciform feel with its centrally placed tower. This was once one stage higher than it is today, very pleasant, yet distinctively squat, charmingly capped with its seventeenth-century wooden and leaded bell cupola. Further verification of a drastic change in size and proportion can be noted in the outline of a once massive chancel arch clearly visible on the external west face of the tower well above the present roof line, yet there is nothing in the history or documentation to explain the reason for this shrinkage.

An evolution in three distinct stages is suggested with first a

Norman cruciform building followed by the very early thirteenth-century medieval twin-aisled design that was probably deemed necessary to house a growing congregation, and finally the building we see today, with its absent north aisle and heavy 1835 restorations. Much is conjecture but the tower is essentially early Norman, with window insets that are typical of the Early English style that pervades the whole south side of the church and the chancel, while the modest porch is in the later Perpendicular style and appears as almost an afterthought, placed as it is at the extreme west end of the building. On entering one is greeted by what remains of a painting of St Christopher on the wall opposite and the interior has a number of other interesting features to be seen, not least of which is a very rare floor piscina at the foot of one of the columns, the like of which can be seen nowhere else in Norfolk. A clumsily altered Royal Coat of Arms features the arms of the Jacobite dynasty (1603–89) with the initials of George III painted on to them without any regard to proper heraldry and over the now cramped arch into the tower hang two original Decalogue boards.

There is also a large memorial carved with an abundance of cherubs, helms and coats surmounting a sheet knotted at both ends and containing a rather gruesome collection of carved skulls and human bones. This commemorates one Robert Blyford and his wife, who died in 1672 aged just thirty-five, while he lived on as a widower until he was seventy in 1702. All that can be said of this family is that they must have been very wealthy to have such a grand monument yet nothing in their history suggests any other claim to fame.

The nave

ALL SAINTS CARLETON RODE

Golden in the late afternoon sun of autumn, this seems a very grand church for such a relatively small secluded village. This is not a place of historically famous families, nor did it ever take centre stage in the course of history; nevertheless it stands as proud as many that have.

Built in the Decorated style typified by its west window, the massive stone tower appears something of a conundrum, until it is revealed that in the early eighteenth century it was in a ruinous state and emergency repairs had to be made in 1717. Despite this, the south-east buttress collapsed into the church in 1755 and further repairs completely changed the original shape of the tower forever. Much of the rest of the building is from the Perpendicular period although the porch may be a little earlier. The nave and clerestory are high pitched, allowing for some fine Tudor windows in the aisles, particularly the enormous one in the north aisle that climbs mightily from just three feet above the ground. Pevsner describes the chancel as 'lavish' and for some reason verifies its date by the presence of a single piece of stained glass, a trefoil panel of a seated figure on a dark blue background in the south window. Even without the glass to corroborate the chancel is clearly thirteenth-century, as is the priest's doorway. Four bay arcades with double, hollow, chamfered arches supported by octagonal piers, increase the stature of the building, balancing it beautifully.

The interior is spacious and lofty, mixing the old with new without embarrassment. It is fairly rare to find two separate piscinas yet this church boasts three, a beautifully carved thirteenth-century double piscina in the sanctuary, a single piscina dating from the fourteenth century in the south aisle and yet another fourteenth-century example in the north chapel. All that remains of the rood screen is the base painted with the twelve apostles, each with his own symbol, the style of the figures being more rustic but still reminiscent of the famous paintings at Ranworth. Painted on the walls, six crosses, used ceremonially on the day the church was first consecrated, have survived the destruction and turmoil of changing religious thought for over six hundred years.

ST MARGARET CLEY-NEXT-THE-SEA

The sea beat a retreat from here long ago, leaving Cley no longer quite as 'next-the-sea' as once it was. Looking towards nearby Wiveton across open grassland it is difficult to imagine that this was once the location of a thriving sea port which brought the prosperity needed for a parish church of such cathedral-like scale. Standing beneath vast skies on top of a natural mound, it holds a position as near to perfection as one is likely to see, and even today St Margaret appears master of all it surveys. How much more so must it have been to a medieval mind?

The slightly incongruous tower is early thirteenth century, but most of what we see today is the result of the rebuilding and expansion of an earlier church at the beginning of the fourteenth century. The rebuilding program began under the patronage of Lady Petronella and Lady Maud, heiresses of the wealthy de Vaux family and, while not a certainty, it is likely that the design was the brainchild of a master mason belonging to the architecturally talented Ramsey family, who were responsible for much of Norwich Cathedral and Westminster Palace. Clearly further work was intended, but the majority of the building was complete when the Black Death struck in 1349, bringing a temporary but prolonged halt to all further work. After the devastation of the plague subsided, work resumed once again, but eventually the Reformation, the retreating sea and the demise of the port brought hard times and an end to the church's period of upward mobility.

The massive Perpendicular style south porch features an impressive array of carved heraldic shields dating from the beginning of the fifteenth century. Among the notables represented are the de Vaux, de Roos, de la Pole and Mortimer families as well as Richard II, all of which must have added gravity to a place where, in addition to its religious functions, acted as the customary place for all manner of legal, communal and domestic transactions. The pageantry continues into the interior, where there are misericords carved with further coats of arms and devices, including that of the honourable Grocers Company which was given in 1532.

A large, luminous interior features a highly idiosyncratic clerestory made up of cinquefoil windows, the light from which falls upon wonderfully carved corbels supporting the niches at the top of the arcade pillars, some bearing traces of their original colouring. Cavorting musicians, animals and a delightfully rustic St George and the Dragon are all carved with a humour reminiscent of characters

The font

painted by Brueghel. A bevy of bench ends continue the sense of mischief, with carved poppy heads, faces, some with tongues stickling out, and a mermaid, all giving an amiable ambiance to this profoundly human interior.

Peppered around the floors are a number of brasses, several depicting groups of half a dozen figures, some almost complete, some fragmentary but all extremely interesting. The pulpit is dated 1611 and the seven-sacrament font, although heavily defaced by iconoclastic brutishness, retains enough of its imagery for its lessons to be clearly interpreted.

Having thoroughly explored the interior it is well worth another walk around the outside. The cheeky enthusiasm of the carving throughout the interior is grandly juxtaposed to the intricacy of the carved tracery of the windows, which are truly beautiful, and the elegance and style of the building as a whole further encapsulates not only the skill but the belief of the craftsmen who created this lovely church.

nave

ST MARY CRANWICH

This is the last place you might expect to find such a perfect example of a Saxon round tower church: tucked away down a tiny lane hidden behind a lay-by off a major road.

It stands on a pre-Christian site in a very rare example of the round graveyard favoured by the early Saxons (probably inspired by the far more ancient practice of burial mounds). The slim round tower, the base of which may date from as early as AD 700, abuts a tiny nave and chancel. Both have had their slate roofs replaced with Norfolk reed thatch in 1973, but it is likely that the slates had been a more recent roofing material and that the original roofs were once thatch.

Apart from the occasional hiss of tyres on tarmac speeding past in the distance the feeling here is that little has changed for centuries. The tower, as might be expected for such an early example, tapers irregularly towards the top, where it is crowned by thirteenth-century battlements and unique soundholes that appear to have been modelled out of single pieces of stone, with a tracery design described by Mortlock as looking like 'cub-scouts knots'. The fourteenth-century south porch, although in reality quite small and entirely rustic in design, gives the impression, because of the petite scale of the rest of the building, of being almost massive. Windows throughout vary greatly in period with the date of some open to debate but some in the nave in the Perpendicular style can be accurately dated to the period between 1350 and 1400.

Inside simplicity prevails; plain nineteenth-century plastered ceilings and whitewashed walls seem entirely appropriate. And with a font dating from around 1300, a very attractive piscina from the same date, a much earlier south door, traces of two consecration crosses and a Hanoverian Royal Arms, rare in that it is painted in monochrome, all is just as it should be. A perfect little gem.

The monument to Reverend John Partridge and the Ten Commandments and Lord's Prayer plaques.

ALL SAINTS CROSTWIGHT

Like so many other Norfolk churches, Crostwight lies tucked away among fields in a setting that could hardly be improved upon; medieval architects were often masters at choosing the setting for their buildings, often disregarding the distance from its village or settlement.

Having once fallen into a piteous state, this church has, thankfully, been lovingly rescued, and just how lucky we are becomes immediately apparent once inside.

The still hefty tower lost its upper part in 1910 when that section had to be dismantled due to its hazardous condition. Mighty buttresses that once climbed in three stages part way up the tower now reach the very top, upon which rests a shallow pitch red tiled roof that looks for all the world as if it is merely resting there for a moment before moving off somewhere else. The thatched chancel is now in excellent condition and a robust full, square porch set against the nave blends the whole beautifully. In their excitement to get to the interior, reference books spend little time describing the exterior and although this is perhaps understandable it still a very interesting building.

It would be reward enough that the large, beautifully radiant interior boasts a lovely fifteenth-century carved screen, as well as a fine thirteenth-century Purbeck marble font. But repairs in 1846 also revealed a cornucopia of medieval paintings. Bearing in mind that this church could easily have been lost forever, the survival of these wall paintings, their extent and content making them possibly the most remarkable in East Anglia, approaches the miraculous in terms of luck. Late fourteenth century or very early fifteenth century in origin, they run along the north wall. At the west end are the Seven Deadly Sins in the form of a tree, then a sequence that Mortlock sees as some sort of morality statement, followed by a huge St Christopher and finally the Passion, starting with the entrance of Christ into Jerusalem, through ten episodes of pictorial allegory and belief, culminating in the Ascension.

ST ANDREW EAST LEXHAM

It is claimed by many that this church was built in AD 900, which would make it the oldest round tower church in England. It is indisputably very old. In the middle of what is now a working farmyard it stands aloof on the crest of its circular churchyard, which was very likely once a pagan burial site. The top of the tower has three distinctly unusual belfry openings that do not in fact pierce the full depth of the tower walls. None of them is the same design style or period and their actual date can really only be guessed at approximately; however, the lancet window on the ground floor of the tower is probably late thirteenth century. Nave and chancel are all in one and, although the outside walls are largely rendered now, long and short work quoins made from stones from Barnack quarry are evident.

North and south doors are early English from around 1200 and the interior is simple, well kept and evidently much loved. In the sanctuary is a fine example of an angle piscina covered by a pretty ogee arch to the front and a half round arch to the side above a dropped sill sedilia. There is reason to believe that there was a wooden church here even before this ancient building giving an unassailable pedigree to this spot which has witnessed English Christianity almost from its inception.

The piscina

ALL SAINTS
EDINGTHORPE

A childhood holiday haunt of the First World War poet and hero Siegfried Sassoon, who adored this lovely little church and the remoteness of the location miles from his native Kent, hidden up a meandering farm track within sight of the coast yet offering far reaching inland views of Norfolk. Today little has changed. What a joy of a place and what a gem of a church.

The remoteness of location is probably the reason there is so much of the original to see on both the inside and the outside of this church; it is a fact that poorer communities, and this tiny backwater can hardly have ever been rich, were often left, by virtue of their lack of money, with a church that retained far more ancient features than more prosperous areas. The tower has an octagonal belfry from about 1400 but debate about the origins of the tower itself is best left to the experts. Mortlock claims it as Norman while others are equally emphatic that, due to the thickness of the walls it is unquestionably Saxon. The rest of the exterior of the building continues with a pretty thatched nave joined by a tiled porch and chancel. Pevsner claims all the windows are of the Perpendicular period only to raise further argument since others claim they range over far more disparate periods.

Let the rivers of debate flow on. I arrived at this magical spot with the early morning light of a beautiful spring day and, whatever other facts may be contested, the breathtaking beauty of the scene cannot. Standing there, as it has for at least as long as scholarship eventually agrees, bathed in pink light, amid a fortress of trees, it presented me with what one might call 'a major moment'.

Sometimes a wonderful exterior can lead to the disappointment of a rather less inspiring interior, but not here. Immediately on entering you are greeted by a fine painting of St Christopher on the north wall while further along nearer the chancel, just above the seventeenth-century pulpit, is a rare, lovely, carved and painted statue niche

Above: The painted screen
Above right: The pulpit and painted statue niche
Right: The font

with a traceried head that crowns the old rood stair. And then there is the screen. Its entrance to the chancel is surmounted by two beautifully carved wheels of intricate rose tracery with the lower side panels depicting six saints and their symbols: Bartholomew a knife, Paul a Bible and a sword, Catherine a Bible and palm frond, James the Great a staff and scallop shell, Andrew a cross and Peter keys, all painted in a pre-1400s style. An interesting, probably apocryphal, tale is that the numerous small holes in the panels were caused by the bullets of Roundhead soldiers who took pot shots at it.

An octagonal font has, mounted on the wall behind it, what is left of the original door to the church which demonstrates well the ravages of time. All in all there is little to fault this lovingly tended little church.

ST MARY FISHLEY

An enchanting little church kept a closely guarded secret by its camouflage thicket of pines, oaks and limes. Isolated yet barely a mile from busy Acle, the eastern aspect gazes out over rolling countryside and the marshes. A Norman tower according to some, but claimed as Saxon by the Round Towers Society who place the date in the arena of 800–1000, is unusually narrow with a later brick top. The south door is unquestionably Norman with a billet frieze, alas rather severely restored, along with much else, in 1861. The remainder of the church is thirteenth or fourteenth century in origin and it is just possible that there was once a north aisle. There is little to speak of in the interior, and it has been commented that, no matter how remote or poor the congregation might have been, there must have been some hatchments, monuments, altar tombs or ledger slabs at one time, so why and when did their comprehensive removal take place? Be that as it may, what the interior may lack in interesting content is fully compensated for, to all who beat a path to its door, by the truly lovely position this building occupies.

ST ANDREW FRENZE

This is not to be found where you might expect it to be, and asking directions is of little avail since very few local people seem to know of its existence. This small gem, standing on a mound, among a cluster of farmyard buildings, is reached by way of a practically obscured turning off of the main road from Diss to Scole. Eminently worth the search, the tiny church, beautifully maintained by the Churches Conservation Trust, is a treasure, the key to which can be obtained from a most obliging keyholder at Frenze Hall directly opposite. Being tucked away like this has probably been its blessing, ensuring that over the centuries it suffered little damage from inconclastic vandals who destroyed whenever and whatever they could easily find.

The first known Lord of the Manor was John de Lowdham around 1280 and it is assumed that the church dates from about then. This is not another example of a collapsed tower – there never was a tower, just a simple bellcote on the nave roof. The chancel no longer exists as it was pulled down in the nineteenth century. The exterior has a fascinating and charmingly rustic ambience but it is what has been preserved within that is really interesting. This is reached through a Tudor brick porch with a quaint pinched footed arch leading to an interior, which, although very simple, has a fourteenth-century octagonal font, an interesting Jacobean pulpit with matching family pew and a rare framed, Royal Arms of James I, plus a unique family history told in brasses.

Through marriage the presiding de Lowdham family became the Blennerhassetts, a name that the tetchy Sir John Paston made fun of in a letter dated 1473, stating 'Raff Blaundrehassett wer a name to styrte an hare'. Strange name notwithstanding, this family is remembered in a series of ten memorial brasses, mostly intact and spread throughout the church. They are Ralph Blenerhassett (d.1475), John (d.1510), his wife Jane (d.1521), their son Thomas (d.1531), his wife Margaret, Mary (d.1587) and Anne. Unfortunately the brass of her husband George Duke has been stolen. There are two further brasses, Johanna Braham (d.1591), thought to be Margaret's mother, and a shroud brass of Thomas Hobson (d.1520). Measuring from eleven inches to about two foot six, and showing the figures in armour and costume spanning a long period, several are what is known as palimpsest brasses, brasses that have been turned over and reused from much earlier brasses taken from elsewhere, in this case almost certainly the shrine of St Edmund at Bury after it burnt down in 1463.

The family finally died out in 1636 when the estate was bought by one Richard Nixon. It is interesting to note that in 1736 it was recorded that sixty people lived here in six houses, a population that has never been anything like that since.

Above: The memorial brasses
Below: The pulpit

ST MARY GISSING

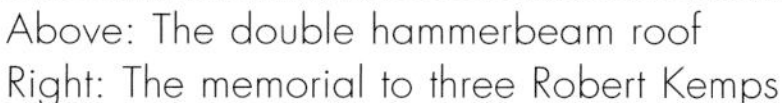

Above: The double hammerbeam roof
Right: The memorial to three Robert Kemps

Pevsner questions whether this is a Saxon round tower or not but no one else does, and judging by the splayed windows half way up the tower it is pretty likely that it is, as claimed, a Saxon tower dating somewhere between the early tenth and mid eleventh centuries. What is certain is that the Normans added the belfry windows to the tower and the two-light windows on the west side carry their classic zigzag carved decoration. The claim that part of the nave is also Saxon is not so easy to substantiate but perfectly possible. The south doorway is once again classic Norman and appears to have been the original entrance until the north porch was built in the fifteenth century. Prettily decorated with flowers in the spandrels and crowns and fleurons climbing up the arch, this porch is quite large considering the size of the church and once had a room above the doorway.

Once inside the eye is immediately drawn up to the splendid double hammerbeam roof with its host of angels, wings outstretched. Its colouring is darker than usual but once the eye has adjusted to the light conditions its beauty is revealed in full; it too seems very large and grand for the size of the church. The north chapel is early fourteenth century divided from the rest of the church by a Jacobean screen. This is the family chapel of the Kemps, who were Lords of the Manor here from 1324 until the early twentieth century. The walls are festooned with their memorials; although none of them has figures they are of varied design and extremely interesting. Robert seems to have been a chosen Christian name for the dynasty and the elaborate if somewhat verbose plaques sing the praises of at least three Robert Kemps having died in 1614, 1710 and 1734. The last Kemp to be buried here was Colonel Sir Kenneth Hager Kemp in 1936.

ST ANDREW GUNTON

Above: Exterior from the east. Right: The chancel. Below: The organ.

This is the only building in Norfolk designed by Robert Adam. It was commissioned by Sir William Harbord in 1769 to compliment his new house that lies only a few hundred feet from the church. This is a masterpiece of simplicity, resembling nothing so much as a very fashionable folly. This is a surprisingly deep church in proportion to its width, with four large niches running along the sides just above ground level and four squared windows above. A beautifully calm interior continues the simplicity of the whole.

This is a difficult church to get to, however, since it lies in the heart of a 1000-acre private estate, but it is a rich reward to those who persevere. It is now in the care of the Churches Conservation Trust, who look after it with their normal care and flair.

ST MARY HADDISCOE

The porch, St Mary Haddiscoe

In this area the delineation between counties has moved back and forth several times over the centuries. Nowadays this is definitely Norfolk but a sneeze could easily blow you into Suffolk. The River Waveney snakes lazily along here and two very fine round tower churches practically overlook each other across the Haddiscoe marshes.

Mention Norfolk round towers and most people will rhapsodise about Haddiscoe, yet many will never have given a thought to its older but less famous neighbour, a stone's throw away at Thorpe. There is certainly debate as to the exact date of the tower at Haddiscoe. Saxon or Norman? The only thing that is not disputable is that the tower at Thorpe is definitely Saxon and an earlier construction than its neighbour. The tower at Thorpe shows signs of it having been constructed with an eye on defence or hiding, and both towers had crenulated parapets with chequered patterns added in the fifteenth century. The nave at Thorpe is thatched and possibly Saxon while the nave at Haddiscoe is grander and

ST MATTHIAS
THORPE-NEXT-HADDISCOE

sits under a tile roof. The porch at Thorpe is fourteenth century but the presence of a scratch dial on the wall inside it indicates that there was originally only a simple doorway entrance to the church. The porch at Haddiscoe is fifteenth century and leads to an elaborate Norman doorway decorated with a classic zigzag motif and very striking early ironwork on the door itself. Above the door is a very rare piece of, remarkably well preserved Norman sculpture of a seated figure – its survival through centuries of religious bigotry is nothing short of a miracle. Both interiors have architectural features and artefacts worth noting and at Haddiscoe there are the remains of some wall painting.

To visit only one of these lovely churches is to do a disservice to the other, and to miss a unique chance for comparison.

ST MARGARET HALES

We owe much to the Churches Conservation Trust, for without their great work many churches would simply disappear, Hales among them, and what a loss that would be as it is certainly the most complete example of a pre-Gothic Norman church in Norfolk, possibly the whole country. Forgetting the religious points of view for a moment, it never ceases to amaze me that the Government, local business and the populace so often pass the buck on the cost of preserving our historic heritage. Happy to glean the profits generated by tourism they blindly fail to notice that many tourists come to specifically see our historic treasures. Thank God for the Trust, who work tirelessly to preserve and restore, leaving these wonderful buildings open for all to see and charging visitors nothing for the pleasure.

It has to be said that this church suffered from clerical and official greed from very early on; however, in this case it is probably to that greed that we owe the uniquely original state this little church has retained. Once part of the benefice of St Olave's Priory at Herringfleet, originally the income from any land and other assets of St Margaret's went partly to St Olave's and the balance to the incumbent who was responsible for the church's upkeep. In the Middle Ages it was not unusual for the parish funds to be appropriated by monasteries and indeed about 37 per cent of Norfolk livings suffered from this, but Hales was a particularly poor parish. Around 1480 St Olave's decided they wanted all the income and appointed a simple chaplain with no income or responsibility for the upkeep of the building so consequently the church was neglected and at a time when Romanesque chancels were everywhere being rebuilt there was no money available here so all stayed as it was.

A Norman round tower, a twelfth-century apsidal chancel, a thatched roof and not one but two lovely Norman doorways make this a gem of a church. Never possessing a porch the main entrance was the north door and it is so fine an example of a Norman doorway that the great Norwich school painter John Sell Cotman drew it in about 1838. A towerless church existed well before 950 but around 1150 the Normans transformed it, and their masterpiece has to be the north nave doorway. The arch has five heavily ornamented bands, the instantly recognisable zigzag motif and huge fan wheels of other decorative motifs.

Inside there is a lovely, remarkably intact fifteenth-century octagonal font with angels and roses standing on a base of lions under a Jacobean font cover. There is a wall painting of St Christopher, but a far more unusual fourteenth-century painting portraying St James the Great is to be seen behind the eighteenth-century pulpit, while high up in the spandrels of the chancel there are painted angels blowing trumpets.

Above: The chancel
Right: The font
Opposite: The north door

ALL SAINTS HETHEL

The monument to Miles Branthwaite and his wife Mary

This place could never have been that easy to find but in an area now swallowed by the Lotus car company it is very confusing and seems so remote that it is impossible to believe this is only seven miles from the centre of Norwich.

It is more than likely that the square west tower is Norman, the brick pinnacles and embattlements being a later addition. Nave and chancel are in the Perpendicular style but the nave and north aisle have rather unfortunate nineteenth-century windows and a rector restored the chancel with a rather heavy hand in 1737–9. The porch is originally of the same period, although a not unattractive crow stepped brick gable was added in the seventeenth century.

The Branthwaite mausoleum is a major feature of this church and its vaguely baroque shape, executed in red brick, changed the whole design and layout of the building when in 1730 the north chapel was converted for family use. Being a large family, and having gone to all this trouble and expense, it is something of a mystery that only two of the Branthwaite family were ever buried in the vaults, the first being interred in 1740. It is even stranger that the walls bear blank tablets, which, for some reason, never received any inscriptions.

In the chancel there is an earlier, very fine alabaster monument to Miles Branthwaite (d.1612) and his wife Mary. Lying one above the other, Miles on his side resting uneasily on his right elbow and Mary on her back hands clasped in prayer staring up from beneath him. Having made his money from the law he is dressed in legal robes, and she in the expected accoutrements of the wife of a well healed lawyer; under a large hood she wears an elaborate dress with ruffs at the throat and wrists. On the tomb beneath their parents, a son and two daughters kneel on cushions and apart from the hands having been struck off one of the daughters, all the figures are surprisingly undamaged. This may have been one of the advantages of being in a church so remote and difficult to find.

Out in the churchyard there is another interesting feature of this church. The Hethel Thorn is a vast tangled Hawthorn, described in 1864 as having a girth of fourteen feet three inches and said in legend to have been the rallying point for an insurrection in the reign of King John. It is mentioned as a boundary in a deed from the thirteenth century so it is well over seven hundred years old, yet still blossoms every year. There is also an American War Memorial to the men of the 389th Bomb Group who flew from Hethel Airfield during the Second World War; 588 of them were killed in action.

The chancel, All Saints Hethel

THE RED MOUNT CHAPEL KINGS LYNN

The Red Mount Chapel now stands in a very pleasant public park containing other picturesque fragments from about the same period, suggesting that this area was once an important place. Granted a licence to build in 1485, it served as a wayside chapel for pilgrims en route to Walsingham. Pevsner describes this octagonal red brick building, supported at each of the eight angles of the octagon by angle buttresses each pierced by a small arched hole, as 'one of the strangest Gothic churches in England'. It certainly is strange and fascinating. When he visited entry was possible but this is no longer possible so we must rely on his description of the interior. Evidently the upper floors are cruciform in shape and contain the chapel itself plus a small but lavishly vaulted apartment, and the whole structure stands on an oblong tunnel-vaulted basement. No doubt with the right credentials and persistence one could obtain entry but one wonders why such a treasure has not been made more accessible. Nevertheless the exterior presence is still well worth a visit.

ST ANDREW LITTLE
BARNINGHAM

The inclusion of this pretty ordinary church is entirely due a most eccentric and peculiar object inside it. Pevsner gives the whole place a dismissive few lines with no mention of period or style, but as I am always looking for the anecdotal or peculiar angle it earns its place here.

Lying beside the main through road of the village it is reached by a reasonably steep climb up the grass slope that leads to a simple wrought iron gate opening full square onto a square buttressed tower. Built of dressed flint and freestone this church is mainly of very late medieval origin, although records show there was a church here in 1320. The whole exterior was the subject of extensive restoration in the nineteenth century and what older external character it might have had disappeared under the uncompromising hammers of the Victorian restorers. The north door, which is never used, is often called the Devil Door because it is said to have been left open at baptisms for the Devil to leave by, when driven out of the child. Such was the angst of guilt promoted to fearful congregations, that even a newborn child was considered to already be possessed by the Devil, which is not much of a start in life.

The interior is simple to the point of starkness with little more than some pleasant poppy headed bench ends to see, until the eye is swept up the left hand side to the end of the nave and there just in front of the pulpit is an extraordinary box pew. Dated 1640, just a couple of years before the out break of the murderous Civil War, what makes this box pew unusual is the carving on an outer corner. A fairly primitively carved wooden skeleton eighteen inches tall stands in shroud, complete with scythe and hourglass, but even more macabre is that this appears to have been donated for the use of friends and couples getting married. It was carved by a shepherd with the following thought carved around it.

> For couples joynd in wedlock and my friends that stranger is, this seat did I intend built at the cost and charge of Steven Crosbee. All that doe this space pass by, as you are noewe even so was I. Remember death for you must dye and as I am soe shall you be prepare therefore to follow me.

What a cheery chap he must have been. Sadly this is not the original carving, which was stolen in 1996.

The wooden skeleton

ST ANDREW LITTLE SNORING

First sight of this building in the distance is a delight that increases upon closer inspection. A treasure trove of varying period styles coupled with historic whimsy. Around 1800 the tower had a pretty little fairytale conical cap with dormer windows, added, which to my mind, further enhances an already lovely, if somewhat confusing building. The confusion revolves around the fact that, supposedly, within a very short Norman period two churches were built on this spot. Why?

Different schools of thought each offer their own explanation and since the very early Norman or possibly Saxon tower is the oldest remaining part of the building it is perhaps best to start looking for answers there. Standing to the south-west, separated by a mere six feet from the present church the tower is in the slightly spurious position of being the only separated tower in Norfolk – spurious because, unlike the tower at Bramfield in Suffolk, which was never joined to its church, the tower at Little Snoring was definitely attached to a church at once time, albeit not at present. On the side of the tower adjacent to the church porch, a grotesque and threatening carved head glares down from above a classic Norman door, which is set within a huge arch itself below some scant remains of an earlier nave. This hotch potch of styles continues with the entrance porch of the actual church, built around 1300 in the Decorated style favoured then. Once inside, you are confronted by a further piece of the puzzle: another inner Norman doorway complete with traditional zigzag design yet clumsily readapted and fitted into a Gothic pointed arch.

The Norman doorway

In the presence of so many confusing and seemingly contradictory elements, the most feasible scenario for me comes from W.J. Goode's excellent book on round tower churches, in which he posits the simple theory that the timespan between building the first church and its replacement was in fact longer than many people suppose, maybe as much as 150 years, and the reason for an early rebuild was a need for a larger building to accommodate a growing community. The presence of a restrictive stream plus possible subsidence made a new build rather that a mere extension more practical and the incorporation of much of the fabric and material from the original church into the wider and longer building we see today explains many of the incongruities.

We may never know the whole story, yet this remains nevertheless a fascinating building and, to paraphrase Mortlock, the diverse collection of windows alone form a virtual textbook of styles spanning over four hundred years. The interior boasts a very rare arms of James II (rare mainly because he wasn't around long enough for many to appear), a lovely eighteenth-century mahogany pulpit and a fine Norman font. The chancel has Tudor windows on each side and a drop sill sedilia and piscina and a ledger slab between the pews on the south side of the church commemorates a parish priest 'as good perhaps as ever lived'. I left pondering what he could have done to qualify for that damning reservation 'perhaps'.

HOLY TRINITY LODDON

When St Felix brought Christianity to East Anglia, one of the churches he established was at Loddon. The Normans replaced that one and then Sir James Hobart cleared the site and built the present building just before he became Attorney General to Henry VII in 1486. Extremely heavy-handed nineteenth-century restoration has left its mark but was unable to rob the building of its glory. Practically a textbook rendition of the Perpendicular style, the south porch is a jewel. Two storeys high, the lower part with a lovely star-vaulted ceiling, this porch is unusual in having its own substantial turret staircase in the north west-corner. Carving around the base carries up into the spandrels of the entrance, lifting the eye to a canopied niche in which stands a statue of the Trinity, which miraculously managed to escape the attention of Reformation and Puritan sensibility, no mean feat considering its central eye-catching position.

The porch

The nave

Inside there is a rich arch-braced hammerbeam roof and tall seven-bay arcades are cascaded with light from no less that thirty clerestory windows, fifteen on each side. The seven-sacrament font must once have been something but unlike the statue of the Trinity it did not escape and a Mr Rochester from Beccles was paid 6 shillings to destroy its imagery. They certainly got their money's worth, for not a single figure or scene is now identifiable, so enthusiastic was the defacement he carried out. The fifteenth-century rood is most unusual, not only for its colouring but for the fact that that it depicts Biblical scenes, mostly from the life of Christ, rather than the more traditional pictures of individual saints. One of the scenes shows a child spreadeagled on a grid-iron surrounded by turbaned figures. This is St

William of Norwich, the child that the Jews were accused of sacrificially murdering in Holy Week 1144, an accusation that led to massacre and mayhem.

An unusually interesting painting on the wall of the south aisle shows the founder of the church Sir James Hobart and his wife kneeling with the church and a fortified bridge in the background. The inscription states that while he built the church she built the bridge at St Olave's. In the north aisle there is an impressive carved memorial to Lady Dyonis Williamson. Noted for having donated £2000, the largest individual donation made towards the rebuilding of St Paul's after the Great Fire of London in 1666, she also donated a further £2000 to St Mary le Bow and a staggering £4000 to St Dunstan-in-the-East. Sculpted as a reclining figure by Joshua Marshall, she is depicted as a rather masculine-looking old lady, staring into the void as if wondering where to spend her money next.

Some time after photographing this church, at a dinner party far away in Sussex, I met a woman who grew up in Norfolk, at Loddon, daughter of the then vicar. She regaled us with stories of harmless childhood adventures in church and churchyard and the case of the 'mysterious ringing bells' which, she confessed was the result of out-of-bounds trips by herself and a few chosen friends made into the belfry.

The rood screen

ST PETER MELTON CONSTABLE

Standing just inside the gates of Melton Constable Park, is an unusual church that is much older that it at first appears. The central tower with its pyramid roof is Norman and a Norman window can still be seen on the north side, although the Norman door in the west wall is, according to Pevsner, Victorian. The fifteenth-century chancel is extremely truncated, giving the building a squat appearance. The colouring of the stone is welcoming but on the whole gives no indication of what the interior holds.

The slightly rustic flamboyance of the interior, complete with a Flemish triptych rederos attributed to Rubens, leans heavily towards the rococo and comes as a surprise after the blunt angles of the exterior. This is a church dominated by memorials of two intertwined families, the Hastings and Astleys. Sir Jacob Astley, the Royalist victor of the battle of Edgehill, is famous for his pre-battle prayer: 'Oh Lord thou knowest how busy I must be this day. If I forget thee, do not thou forget me.' Although not represented among the monuments, he would

The nave and chancel

Stained glass

certainly have worshipped here. The south transept, which forms what is known as the Hastings pew, was built in 1681 and is approached from the nave by a short flight of stairs dated 1636 on the newel post. The walls are festooned with family memorials of varied merit. One, that of Sir Phillip Astley (d.1779) and his wife, has large portrait medallions; another, that of Lady Stanhope (d.1812) high up on the south wall, carries a full-size shrouded female figure draped above it, while two sad little plaques commemorate Richard and Louisa Maria, children of Sir Edward Astley and Dame Anne Astley. The little boy died aged three and the girl aged just sixteen months.

Although left open for all to enter, few locals even knew of it when asked, and it is not somewhere you might stumble upon so there is a touch of the private chapel about this extraordinary little church.

The south transept

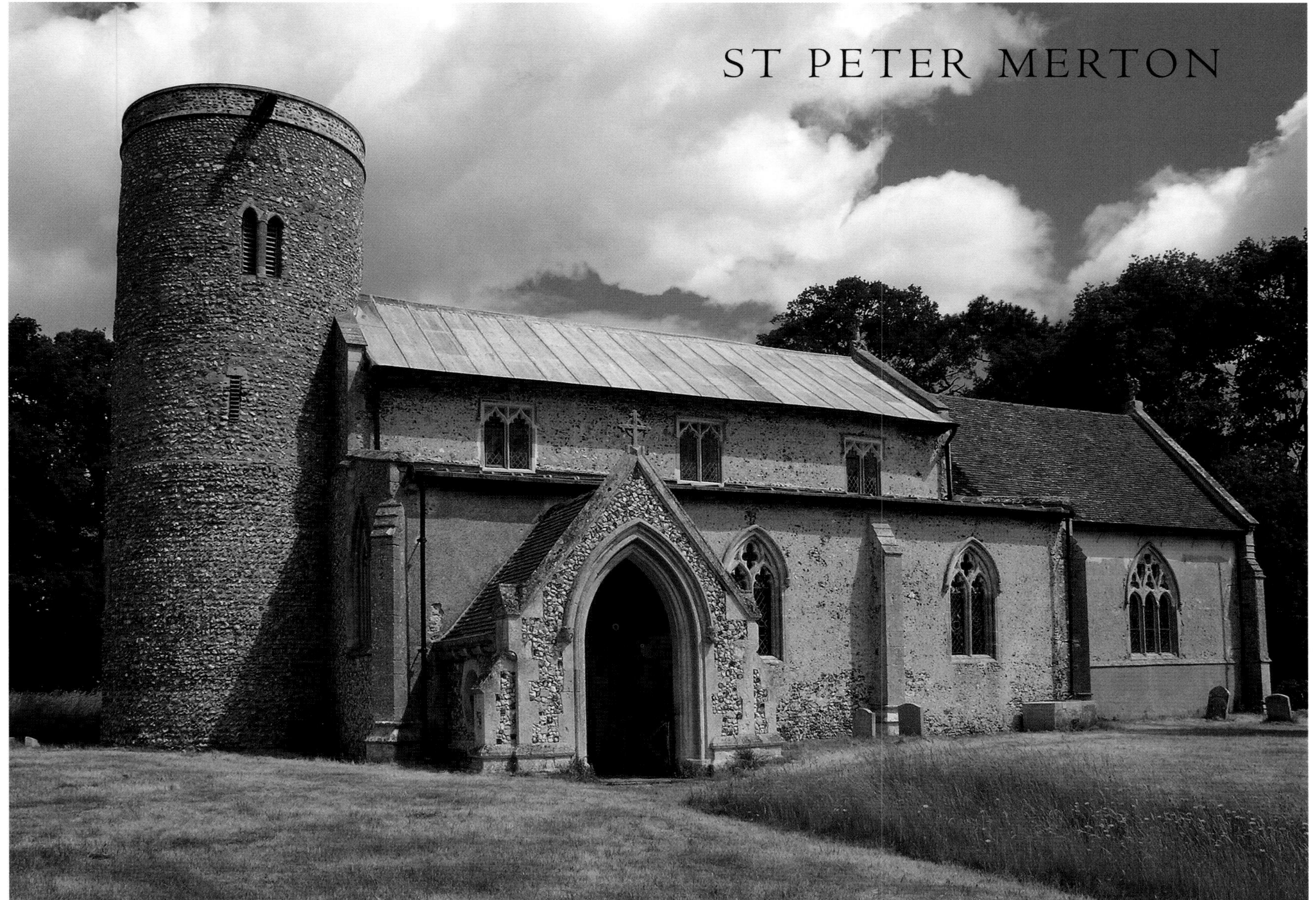

ST PETER MERTON

Beautifully set in the parkland of Merton Hall, this fine round tower church has ancient origins. The lower part of the tower is almost certainly pre-Conquest, rising to an early Norman finish with two-light bell openings. The impressive nave and chancel are mainly fourteenth century, the nave being heightened and a single-sided clerestory added in the fifteenth century. Two porches, a south and a Perpendicular style north which faces a lake, lead to an interior with a very fine two-light screen dated around 1430 and an excellent sedilia and piscina from the early fourteenth century. An unusual six-sided font from the fifteenth century must have been very impressive before the iconclasts decided to deface it; its tall Perpendicular font cover, although largely restoration work now, still retains its lifting apparatus. There are two good brasses. On the wall Sir William de Grey (d.1495) kneels in full heraldic armour with both his wives, Mary and Grace; behind him kneel five sons and behind their mothers five daughters. Under the carpet is Thomas de Grey (d.1562), also in armour. A Jacobean two-decker reader's desk and pulpit is worth noting, as are the lovely fragments of thirteenth-century glass in the north-east window.

ALL SAINTS NARBOROUGH

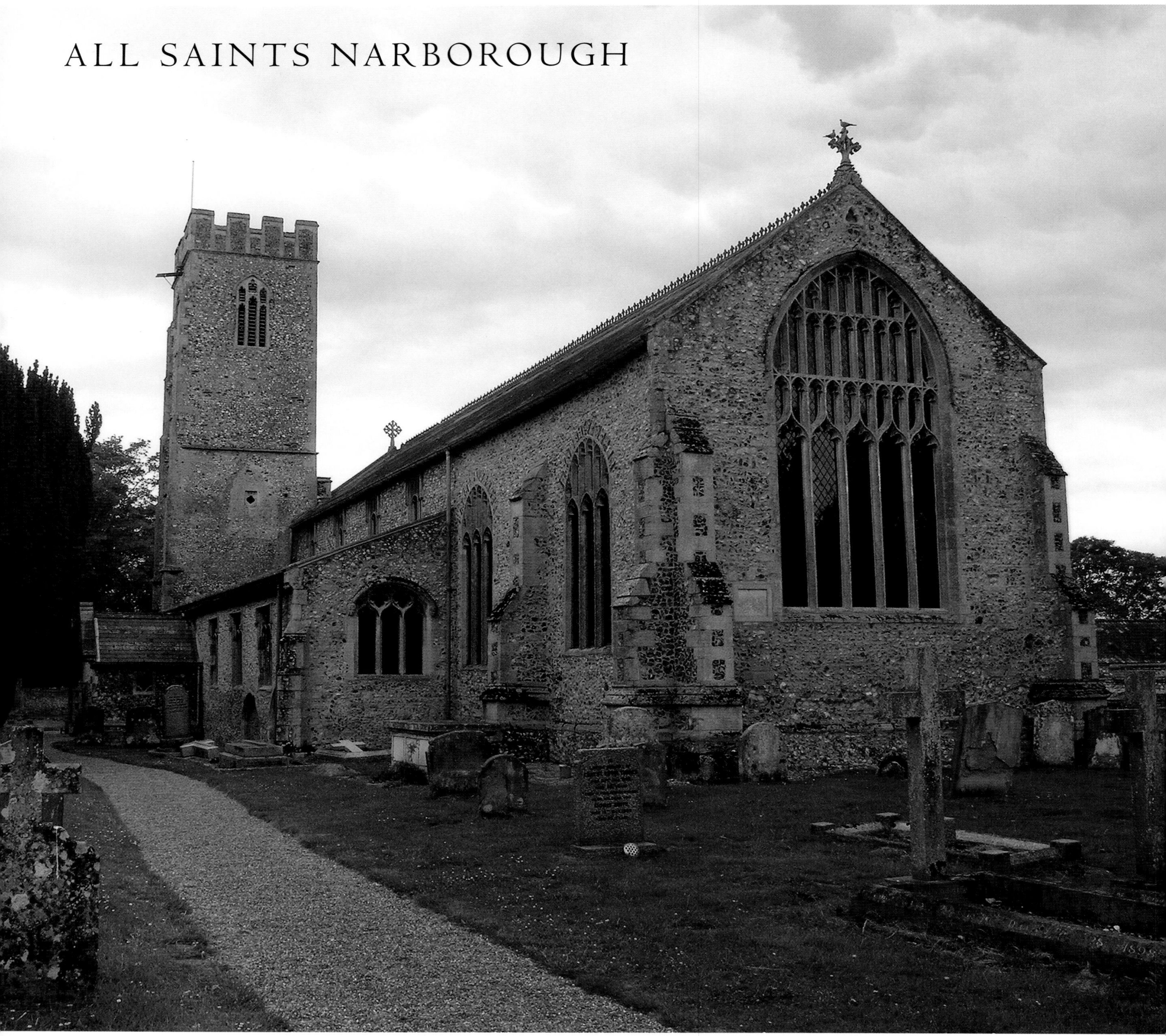

Standing in the middle of the village, this church presents itself as ordinary, but this is misleading. There are traces that suggest Norman origins, but this is primarily a building of the late fourteenth century with a late thirteenth century tower that once had a small spire; this was dismantled in 1679. A sundial can be seen on the buttress of the tower and the belfry houses a single bell made in Thetford in 1607. This is something of a puzzle, since frames for two further bells stand empty, never having had bells. Did the money just run out or did they merely forget to install them?

The light and airy interior has fourteenth-century arcades with light and colour spilling in from the nave clerestory as well as from the large windows of the chancel. But it is the sheer range of the monuments to one family that predominates this place, offering, in brass and stone, a comprehensive view of the Spelman dynasty. On the floor at the north side of the chancel is the brass of Henry Spelman (d.1496), Recorder of Norwich, standing alongside his wife, also another brass for John Spelman (d.1545), a single figure shown in full armour and yet another for John (d.1581), also depicted in full armour. On the north chancel wall is the lovely brass of Sir John Spelman, a judge at the trial of Sir Thomas More who also prepared the case against Anne Boleyn. He is seen in his judge's robes alongside his wife in a dress covered with heraldry. Finally, on the south wall, is the brass of John Eyer (d.1561) with his wife, a widow of one of the Spelmans. As Receiver General Eyer became very wealthy during the Dissolution of the Monasteries and interestingly it would have been him who authorised the tearing up of hundreds of brasses throughout the county. Yet his own brass and those of his family survived. It seems that the principle of double standards is historic.

In a striking stone monument on the north wall of the chancel we find Sir Clement Spelman (d.1607) and his wife, both wearing ruffs, reclining one above the

The monument to Sir Clement Spelman and his wife

other with a child and a baby in its crib in niches higher up. The tomb of Sir John Spelman (d.1662) can be found in the west of the nave while the unknighted Clement Spelman (d.1679), Recorder of Nottingham, stands pompously bewigged and robed on a plinth on the south side of the chancel. He once stood on an eight-foot plinth but in 1865 his coffin was found standing upright inside the plinth, evidently he had insisted on this since he had no wish to be trodden upon. Alas his wishes were then ignored, and the size of the plinth was reduced so he was re-interred horizontally for all to tread on.

As if further remembrance of the family name were necessary, more members of this family are referred to by heraldic devices in the north window.

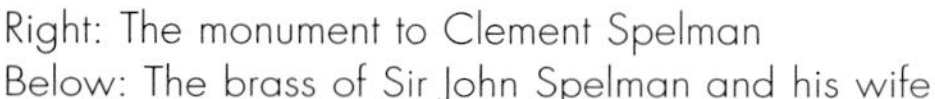

Right: The monument to Clement Spelman
Below: The brass of Sir John Spelman and his wife

ST MARY AND ALL SAINTS NEWTON-BY-CASTLE-ACRE

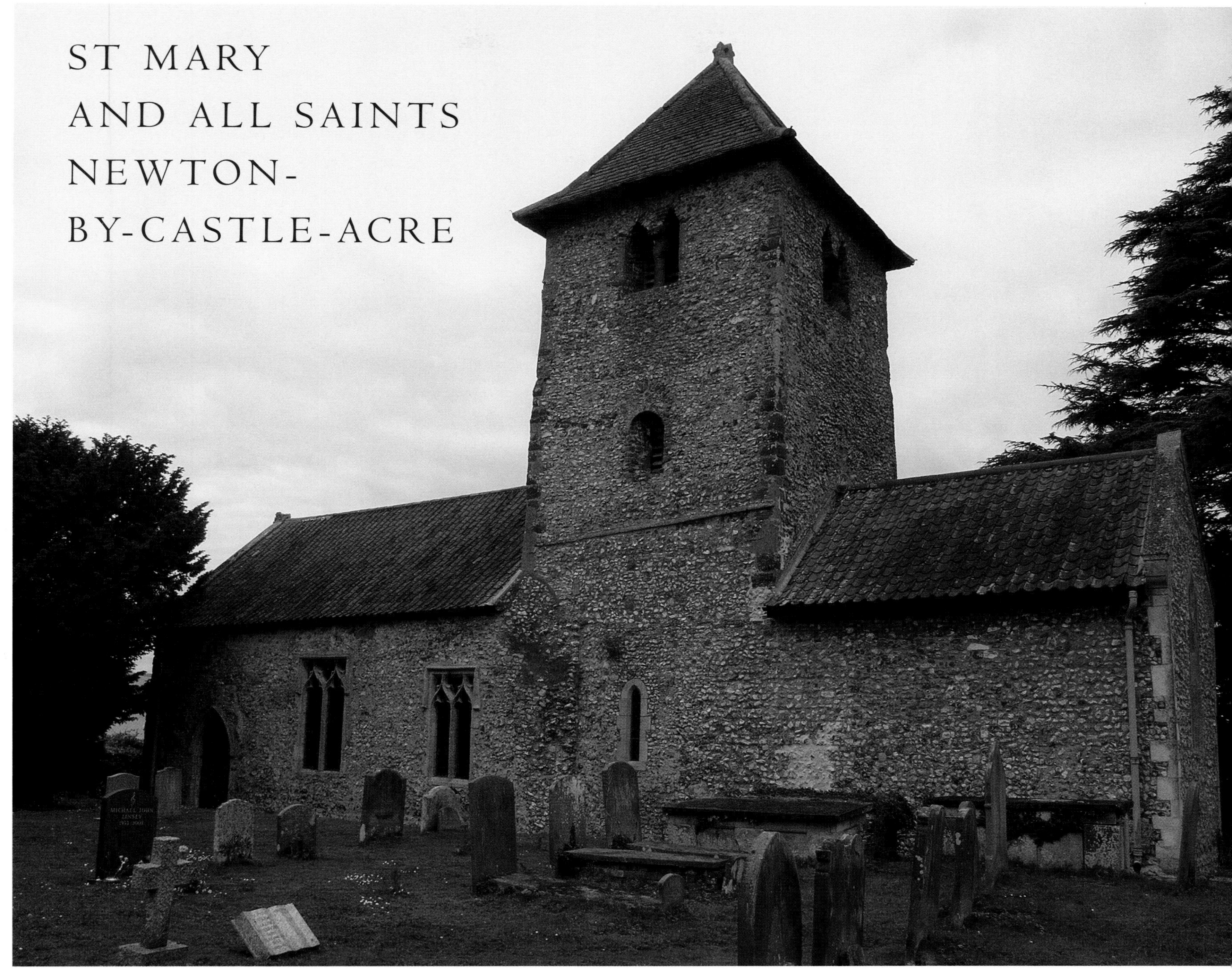

Beside a busy road that nowadays rushes past the village, this lovely church owes its charm to the fact that the village was bypassed by the prosperity that visited most of Norfolk in the fourteenth and fifteenth centuries, so this ancient building was never aggrandised from new-found wealth. The centrally placed tower with its pyramid roof is Saxon, with two light belfry windows. The transepts, traces of which can be clearly seen, were in a ruinous state by the eighteenth century and were demolished. So for most of its life this was a cruciform church. The chancel, which Mortlock describes as 'superbly atmospheric', was rebuilt in the fourteenth century with a very unusual

shelf piscina in the east wall and traces of fourteenth-/fifteenth-century wall painting can be seen. A rudely executed but very interesting coat of arms of George III hangs above the chancel arch, interesting because it contains in its second quarter the arms of France. This dates it to before 1801, when, no doubt to the relief of the French and in a probable but ultimately futile attempt to appease Napoleon, the King of England finally gave up the claim to the title of King of France.

The nave

ST JOHN THE EVANGELIST OXBOROUGH

The stunningly beautiful Oxborough Hall, home of the Bedingfield family, descendants of which still live there, is now cared for by the National Trust. Right next to it stands a fascinating building which at first glance could be taken for the romantic ruin of an abbey or other monastic structure. This is, in fact, what remains of the once much larger parish church, drastically reduced in size due to the collapse of the 150-foot tower and spire, which until one morning in 1948 was among the highest in the county. It is a miracle that children playing in the adjacent schoolyard were unhurt and the resulting devastation, although severe, failed to completely destroy the church or its unique terracotta tombs in the Bedingfield chapel. After eight years of redesign, restoration and rebuilding, the church reopened, skilfully adapted to incorporate the partially destroyed and roofless nave with the original chancel and chapel, creating not only a sensitive place of worship with its own unique ambiance, but preserving very important historic treasures.

The will of Sir Edmund Bedingfield, Marshal of Calais, who died at Calais in 1496, stated his wish to be buried in a chapel to be built by his executors within the chancel of the church at Oxborough. The precise date of the building of the chapel is uncertain but his widow Lady Margaret lavishly endowed the chapel in her will of 1513 so it must have been built before then. The Bedingfields were a staunchly Catholic family that remarkably managed to survive the Tudor passion for executions, something of a feat considering that when the young

The ruined nave

Princess Elizabeth came close to the block herself while imprisoned in the Tower of London by her sister Bloody Mary. Sir Henry Bedingfield was Mary's Governor of the Tower, and therefore Elizabeth's jailor. It speaks volumes for his survival skills that after Mary's death he lived on until 1583, through the reign of the violently Protestant Edward and well into the reign of Elizabeth I. The Bedingfields were considered handsome and Elizabeth's predilection for a shapely male leg may have contributed to his survival but his religious conviction must also have been open to discussion since, although always a Catholic, he agreed to be buried according to the last rites of the Protestant church. It seems he was also a pragmatist.

The terracotta monuments are justly famous for their rarity, beauty and quality, and many people claim them as the work of Flemish craftsmen trained in Italy. Carved in bold Renaissance style relief, they now represent an integral part of the building's structure, with Lady Margaret's tomb forming a screen and, by means of its huge arch, an entrance to the chapel; her husband's, under its double sided canopy forms the dividing wall between the chapel from the chancel. Possibly the finest of their kind in England, their nearest equivalent, although less accomplished by far, is to be seen at Layer Marney in Essex, which is hardly surprising since Lord Marney was the brother of Lady Margaret Bedingfield and executor to her will.

Other family tombs in this wonderful chapel include one commemorating both the 17th Sir Henry (d.1657), whose support of the Stuarts cost him three years in the Tower and a Puritan sequestration of his estate, and Sir Henry 1st Baronet (d.1684), who also suffered for both Charles I and Prince Charles, upon whose restoration he received a peerage and the return of the Bedingfield estates, 'from which time to his death he lived a most exemplary life'. The tomb of yet another Sir Henry (d.1704) and his two wives manages to block the east window of the chapel almost completely. Flamboyantly executed in black touchstone and alabaster it has a forbidding skull with a wreath of bays, being carried aloft by swans and cherubs in a hammock of drapery.

Detail of the monument to Sir Henry Bedingfield

The tomb of Lady Margaret Bedingfield

ST MICHAEL OXNEAD

Standing next to the last great house of the Paston family, Oxnead Hall, this church appears as a bit of a hotch potch, which is sad since its connection with that family should perhaps have assured its fabric just a little more care. These are the Pastons of feud, litigation and letter-writing fame, who gave us such an insight into the medieval mind, but the family members represented in this church are from a much later generation of a dynasty that came from nothing. An interesting side note here is an entry in the visitors' book which sadly, if not completely accurately, laments the fact that the 'poor old Pastons who came from nowhere and to so quickly return there', or words to that effect.

The slender square tower, of proportions I have never seen anywhere else, stands on a base which, along with the south door, seems to indicate an original thirteenth-century building, while the sixteenth-century brick east gable suggests the roof was not only replaced but raised, further unbalancing the proportions. The porch is also brick but this time eighteenth century, and this medley of styles gives the whole a disjointed look as if it had grown not from any considered plan but from a series of arbitrary grafts. None of this is enhanced by the poor condition of the building. However, it is the interior that one wants.

Forewarned by the exterior it comes as no surprise that the interior is also slightly scruffy, but in the chancel we light upon the Pastons of Oxnead Hall – first Sir Clement Paston (d.1597). It was he who built the hall while managing to stay in the good books of three consecutive monarchs (no mean feat considering the fate of so many other loyal subjects of the times), the ever-trustworthy Henry VIII called him his 'champion', Bloody Mary called him her 'seaman' and the capricious Queen Elizabeth I, for reasons best known to herself, simply called him 'father'. Carved in alabaster, sporting a well tended beard, he lies in full armour atop a table tomb and kneeling below him, his wife Alice (d.1608) is suitably dressed in black mourning. Apart from the hands having been senselessly lopped off in the name of religious bigotry, this tomb is in excellent condition for, despite the apparent neglect of the rest of the church, it was lovingly restored in 1956. Another Paston is represented by a large but far less impressive monument by Nicholas Stone, on which a completely expressionless bust flanked by putti stares vacantly ahead. This is Katherine, the wife of the fourth Sir William Paston. She died in 1636.

Despite sad evidence of some neglect and decay this is still a church with very interesting historical connections, commendably left open to for all to witness an important part of Norfolk's past.

The tomb of Sir Clement Paston

ST NICHOLAS POTTER HEIGHAM

This is an ancient place, the name coming from the fact that the Saxons and the Romans before them made pots here. Clay was obtained from the pits to the north-west of the village, which in later times were also a source of the bricks so engagingly used in the fabric of this lovely, broadland, round tower church.

Built in an attractive combination of flint and the very distinctive pale pink local brick, the tower was originally thought to be Norman but it is now agreed by the experts that it is largely Saxon. The elegant, battlemented octagonal top dated by Pevsener as fourteenth-century only adds to its character. A further claim is that it was once separated from the main body of the church and used as a beacon, since in those days the sea came in this far, but over the ensuing centuries the sea has receded some three miles. All the roofs are thatched and directly under the higher nave roof is a row of fifteenth-century clerestory windows, which are particularly tall and delicate for a church this size, making for a wonderfully light interior.

Entry is through a tall porch which once housed the village school in its upper floor. Both aisle walls show much evidence of wall paintings but only in the south aisle can the subject matter – the Seven Works of Mercy – be confirmed with any certainty. The rood screen is well carved with a rood beam still *in situ*, but most peculiarly the clear outline of the original rood group figures can still be seen on the wall of the chancel arch, from where they were savagely wrenched away during the Reformation. It is strange that they were left like this rather than painted or plastered over as most others were. An extremely unusual and interesting fifteenth-century font is constructed entirely of the same local bricks that are used to great effect throughout the building, and – something I have never seen before – high up in the roof beams is a carved wooden pulley that must have been used to raise and lower the font cover, which has long since disappeared.

This is a region steeped in folklore and legend, and locals will regale you with a tale, especially over a glass of something stronger than water, of a young bachelor from nearby Bastwick who in May 1742 was tricked into marriage with a love potion to Evelyn, daughter of Lady Carew. After the wedding, as the party left the church. the bishop and his retinue turned to skeletons and carried off the bride in a coach driven by a skeleton dressed in bishop's robes. But as it crossed Potter Heigham bridge it turned over and fell into the river, and to this day a ghostly clatter of hooves can often be heard on the bridge.

The font

The nave

ST HELEN RANWORTH

There is little point in my doing much more than try to encourage those who have not visited this church, known as the cathedral of the broads, to put it on their priority list. The late fourteenth- and early fifteenth-century exterior replaced an earlier building but merits little space here except to mention the lovely view of Ranworth Broad from the top of the tower. It is not the exterior but the famous rood screen and paintings, enthused about in nearly every book on English churches, that are the glory of this church. In awe, I will merely quote the report from the Society of Antiquaries, as did the normally very descriptive Mortlock: 'The magnificent painted rood screen and reredoses of the nave altars form a composition which is unequalled by any now existing in a district famous for its screens. As a whole, it

The reredos of one of the nave altars

may be said there is nothing of the sort remaining to equal it in England.' If anything, that veers towards understatement.

The paintings have been dated to the late 1400s but there is still debate as to the influence in style. Is it Spanish, German or Flemish? It will suffice to note that these lively, almost vivacious figures with faces so extraordinarily full of expression, when compared with many a vacant look in the secular paintings of that time, is a wonder. It must be remembered that this is not the entirety that would have confronted the medieval viewer. The screen, stretching the full width of the church, extending to form the reredoses of both side chapels, would originally have been topped by an immense and very beautiful rood group – the Crucifixion flanked by the Virgin Mary and St John. Alas this was destroyed in the sixteenth century on the grounds of idolatry by England's earlier version of the Taliban. Overwhelming today, the effect of these paintings on medieval peasants can only be imagined. The paintings were expertly and sympathetically restored by a Miss Plummer and her assistants in 1975 but I will not go into detail and description of them since there is an excellent booklet for sale in the church.

Left: A detail of the rood screen
Right: The nave

The best initial view of this church is from a high seat, carved by some thoughtful soul from a tree stump very near the entrance to the churchyard and climbing up the carved steps into its very comfortable seat is a very rewarding experience.

This is a Norman round tower with a fourteenth-century polygonal top and, very unusually for a round tower, a staircase turret on its south-eastern side. The chancel was rebuilt in 1909 but we are very lucky that there is still a thatched nave, as it was badly damaged in 1948 while rubbish was being burnt in the churchyard. The entrance is through the Decorated north porch, the brick repairs to which are dated 1624. The interior owes much to a less fortunate church in the ghost village of Tottington that lies within the military battle area that has absorbed several beautiful, important, but now sadly off-limits Norfolk churches. Take, for instance the fine lofty, ogee-headed rood screen with its one-light divisions, which was brought to Rockland from Tottington in 1950. The parapet of the rood loft also comes from there, as does the Jacobean pulpit and most of the wonderful benches, joyously carved with poppy heads and a menagerie of mythical animals, including a bear in a head halter, a griffin and other less identifiable flights of the carver's imagination. So one church's loss is another church's gain and we must be grateful that these treasures have all been saved, albeit in a new home, and what better new home than this lovely round tower church?

The carved seat

ST PETER
ROCKLAND ST PETER

ST PETER AND ST PAUL SALLE

As the 126-foot tower looms into sight across sweeping fields it is immediately obvious that this mighty church is of major significance. Wool wealth gave Salle (pronounced Saul) an important part in the story of Norfolk. Arms on a line of shields above the west door are those of Henry V while he was still the Prince of Wales, establishing a date of 1400–13, which is confirmed by an inscription in the glass of the south window, referring to Thomas Boleyn who died in 1411. In addition, a will confirms that the south transept certainly existed in 1444. Before entering, note the unusual carved angels in the spandrels above the west door of the tower. Hovering beneath the arms of various benefactors of the church, such as the Briggs, Beaupré and Rokewood families, they are covered in feathers, which makes them look more pagan than Christian. It is a mystery that they have survived when right next to them empty statue niches testify iconoclastic destruction of far less provocative statuary. The west door, like most of the other doors in this church, is original. Immediately facing you is the towering font cover, which hangs from a massive bracket projecting from the tower. The seven-sacrament font, one of thirty-nine in existence, all but two of which are in Norfolk and Suffolk, bears an inscription asking that we pray for the souls of Thomas Luce, his wife, and Robert Luce their son, chaplain. The nave roof is arch braced, with angels at the intersections, the rafters still retaining decoration and sacred monograms, but the roof of the chancel is more spectacular. Built between 1440 and 1450 it is borne heavenward by an army of fabulously carved angels, of which 159 of the original 276 are still intact. Since the upper part was crudely sawn off in the sixteenth century, only the lower part of the chancel screen remains, with painted panels depicting eight saints, the others coloured but left blank, and parts of the three-tier pulpit still retain some early colouring. Also to be seen are a very fine set of misericords, those to the north depicting animals and those to the south human heads.

Above: The font
Below: The chancel screen

There are many brasses, including that of Geoffrey and Anne Boleyn, the great-great-grandparents of Henry VIII's ill-fated wife, and a fine example of a bracket brass in the north transept of Thomas Roos (Rose), his wife and twelve children. It was from his wool profits that the north transept was built, but an interesting side note to this is to be found in the Cawston Court Roll of 1425. His apparent wealth did not put him above the law – for an entry states that 'Thos Rose grazed 500 sheep on Causton common where he ought not to graze more than 200.' There is so much to see in this church that it is best allow for a very long but thoroughly rewarding visit.

ST MARGARET AND ST REMIGIUS SEETHING

This is a Norman round tower church with a dedication one doesn't see every day. The tower has been patched, repaired and reinforced in numerous places over the centuries, tilting and tapering in an alarming fashion towards a brick top and a spike spire that appears to be trying to hide. It cannot fail to remind us of how many collapsed church towers are to be seen in Norfolk. Much as early builders are generally to be venerated, not everything worked out entirely as they said it would, confirming that the jerry builder is not a modern phenomenon. Many a sermon delivered here on a stormy day must have fallen on the ears of a congregation whose minds were giving more than a passing thought as to whether somewhere other than the church might be a better place to be that day. That said, if the quality of building work might leave something to be desired the overall beauty of the building is indisputable. In fact the unintended serpentine quality of the tower, while probably inspiring angst in the heart of the building standards enthusiast, adds more than a little je ne sais quoi to the building as a whole.

Built in the Decorated style, the nave and chancel are pierced with a variety of windows spanning a number of other periods and on the lower western face of the tower there is also a fourteenth-century window with a bricked up wafer oven beneath it.

A thatched nave joins the chancel, which is less attractively roofed with tiles, although this too may once have been thatched. The south porch has an arch-brace roof and unusual patterned panelling on the south door looks like linenfold but can't be, as the door is of a much earlier date for that style of decoration.

The interior is surprisingly spacious and bears treasures that make all thought of quirky building practice disappear – a cornucopia of fourteenth-century wall paintings. Norfolk abounds in fine church painting and these must certainly stand high on the list. Immediately upon entering there is St Christopher in his traditional position convenient for the passing traveller to pop in and seek a quick blessing from the doorway. Above the pulpit St John the Baptist points an accusatory finger, while on the opposite wall Satan and his hordes of devils are pushing the dammed into hell via purgatory. Further paintings throughout depict the Three Quick and the Three Dead and the life of Christ, consisting of the Annunciation, Nativity, Resurrection, Asscension and Coronation of the Virgin. To the mainly illiterate congregation at the time these pictures were painted, this church must have filled them with wonder, much as the picture palaces did the populace in the early twentieth century. I chose not photograph of them because I felt that would be like revealing the plot of a film I had seen. They should be viewed in person in this, their very own medieval cinema.

ST MARY SHELTON

A lasting impression of this beautiful building is one of cascading colour. Externally as well as internally, all is colour. I approached as the winter sun glanced upon the walls, and the combination of flint tower, red brick porch and walls surmounted by dressed stone clerestory, seemed to glow. Inside the colour rippled as light flooded through some of the most beautiful donor stained glass in the county.

Built in the Perpendicular style of the fifteenth century, on the site of a much earlier church, of which the flint tower, the west window of the south aisle and the font are all that remain, the new design was precisely specified by the donor, the wealthy High Sheriff of Norfolk Sir Ralph Shelton, who paid for all the work as a place for his soul to be prayed for and the eternal glorification of his name. Unfortunately he did not live to see it finished and although he left sufficient funds to complete the project to his exact original plan, his son, Sir John Shelton, was less enthusiastic and it was never completed as Sir Ralph had wished. This lovely place nonetheless played an important role in

The east window

history, for Sir John Shelton was married to Anne Boleyn's aunt and after the execution of that ill-fated queen he and his wife were made guardians of the young Princess Elizabeth, who lived with them at Shelton. Legend has it that they once hid her in the church tower, thus avoiding her arrest and almost certain execution.

Everywhere you look the Sheltons are present, Sir Ralph and his wife can be seen in the upper portion of the central window and Sir John and Lady Shelton are the large kneeling figures in the glass of the east window in the south aisle. Magnificent glass is set into the beautifully delicate tracery of most of the windows and small figures carry the Shelton arms and the bull of the Boleyns. Beneath a much-lowered ceiling are corbels carved with stone angels carrying heraldic shields bearing the letter R, scrolls, and a shell and tun (barrel), motifs that are echoed in the windows. The corbels are alas redundant, for in an act of unbelievable vandalism, the original roof was removed in the eighteenth-century to re-roof a nearby tithe barn.

In the south-east corner of the church is a more primitive work, retaining much of its original sombre colouring. Beneath an extremely crudely painted skull and crossbones, four dwarf figures – father, mother, son and daughter – kneel on top of an heraldic table tomb, defiantly out-staring each other. This is the tomb of Sir Robert Houghton (1623) and it is ill at ease among so much finer work. Above the tower arch, however, is a rare and very fine Royal Arms of William III; carved from oak and painted and gilded, it has no trouble holding its own against so much beauty.

Shelton is part of the Hempnall Group, eight remarkable medieval churches within a short distance of each other, all controlled by one very pro-active team. As well as places of deeply felt religious belief, these churches are beautiful, historic statements of our heritage and each one offers the warmest of welcomes to all visitors. They are a credit to those that run the group and a clear vision of how things can be.

The north aisle

Stained glass

The tomb of Sir Robert Houghton

The arms of William III

ST GEORGE SHIMPLING

The delicate little spire can be seen in the distance from many different angles but the actual approach to the church is down a very long farm track; the tower seems to grow as you get closer.

Nowadays in need of the two supporting bands of iron that encompass it, this is a Norman round tower with a fifteenth-century octagonal top and eight two-light windows, four of which are bell openings and four flushwork blanks. All of this is crowned with a very fetching recessed shingle spire that was added in 1863. The chancel is thirteenth-century and entry into the church is through a heavily restored but very pretty timber and brick north porch from the sixteenth century. The nave is fourteenth-century, with Perpendicular windows and a lovely arch-braced roof with an exceptionally steep pitch. This was apparently built not long after completion of the nave. The roof is carried on corbels that once had carved faces – now savagely hacked off.

Little remains of the stained glass but high up at the top of the east window of the chancel one can get an idea of what might once have been, as there are some lovely early angels playing lutes and harps. But it is a mark of the relentless fanaticism of Puritan belief that even at this height all the faces of the angels have been scratched out. The traditional fifteenth-century font is set on a base of lions, the bowl surrounded with symbols of the evangelists and demi-figures of angels carrying shields adorned with the instruments of the Passion, all under a seventeenth-century cover.

There are also a number of fifteenth-century poppy-headed benches, which once had figures on the castellated arms, but alas these too must have offended the sensibilities of Puritanism, for every figure has been sawn off. On leaving, note the large mass dial on a south nave buttress.

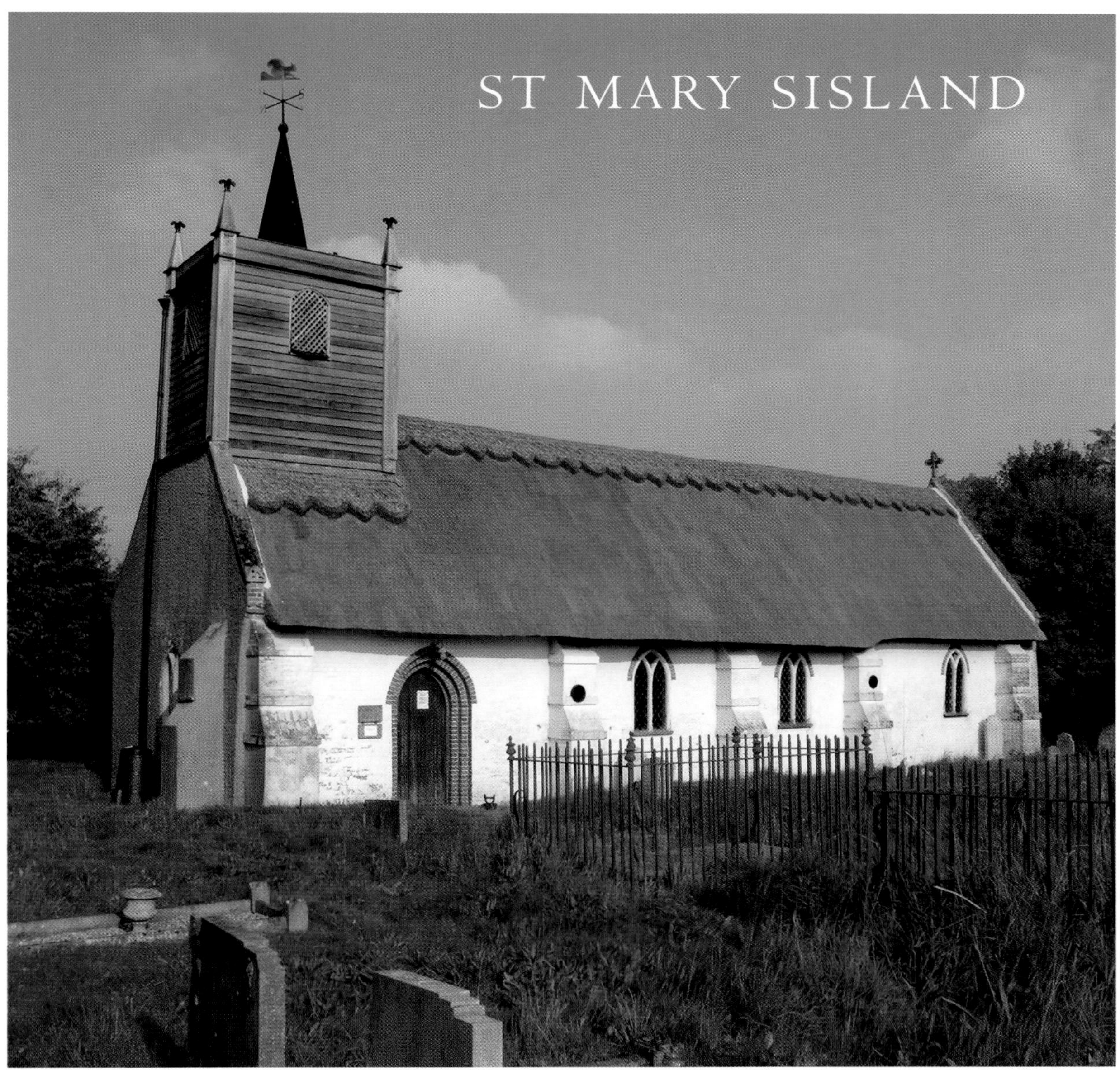

ST MARY SISLAND

This delightful little church, more typical of Essex than Norfolk, was rebuilt in 1761 after the early church that stood just north of present building was destroyed by lightning. Set in a lovely spot next to an old rectory, the nave and chancel are all one under a thatched roof. Whitewash and red brick window copings combine with the pretty little wooden turret, pinnacled and topped by a spirelet and complete with sparkling weathercock resting on the western gable. Simply charming.

The north side of the original church remains left open to the heavens, and a filled-in arch and traceried piscina can be seen. And could the small Y-traceried window beneath the bell turret also be original?

The interior, with plain walls painted white under a plaster ceiling, has a gallery supported on flimsy-looking iron rods at the west end. Fragments of stained glass from the original church can be seen in the roundels of the east window. These show St Peter with his key, St Paul with sword and the Holy Spirit depicted as a dove.

The old font was rescued from the original church and reused. Carved with angels, lions and flowers, it stands on what Mortlock describes as 'a quartet of the snootiest, nose-in-the-air lions you ever saw'.

ST GEORGE SOUTH ACRE

Although this church is overshadowed by a grander and more famous neighbour at Castle Acre, to pass it by, as many possibly do, would be to miss a rare treat. What we see today is a building largely in the Perpendicular style with its earlier thirteenth-century origins clearly visible. This is a church dominated by a family first mentioned in the reign of Henry I, when Sir Eudo de Arsik was Lord of the Manor. The battlemented tower, with its unusually large three-light west window, is built on the foundations of one much older and, as one might expect, it bears the various carved arms of the Harskye family who built it in the fifteenth century.

Through a very early fourteenth-century doorway in the north porch, the interior presents an intriguing mixture of changing religious statement alongside important historic artefacts. Just inside to the right is a chest carved with blank cusped arches and large rosettes. This is the dower chest of Katherine Calthorpe, the wife of the third Sir John Harsyke (d.1384), both of whom are to be seen, touchingly holding hands, in a splendid life-size brass in the chapel. Now relocated to the tower arch, the fourteenth-century screen was once very fine and, although much deteriorated, it is still beautiful. Against the north wall of the aisle lies the effigy of a Knight Templar, thought to be Sir Eudo, who went on crusade to the Holy Land and now lies here, crossed legs resting on a small dog in the traditional manner of Templar tombs. A first glance of the iron-gated chancel chapel reveals a disappointing, although understandable, chain and padlock, but thankfully an address near by where a key can be obtained. It is well worth the short walk, as the chapel contains both the life-size brass referred to earlier and the colourful alabaster and marble monument of Sir Edward Barkham and his wife. They lie beside each other on top of a tomb chest, two kneeling sons and three daughters beneath them. Sir Edward, once Lord Mayor of London, is in armour and civic robes, while all over the monument is a plethora of carved and coloured references to mortality, such as an explicitly grisly charnel house full of broken skulls and bones, a statue of Death as a robed skeleton and empty winged hourglasses, all combining in a virtual festival of the macabre.

The fascination of this treasure of a church is just how much there is to discover and for that very reason I leave you to be explore it further. There is much more to see under its pretty hammerbeam roof.

The tomb of Sir Edward Barkham and his wife

The base of the tomb

ALL SAINTS STANFORD

None but the determined will now see this church, for it lies at the heart of the Thetford battle area, where the army train by constantly shelling somewhere in the vicinity and only with army permission and during a prolonged lull in the cannonade is it possible to visit it. As my namesake I desperately wanted to see it and I got my wish on my second attempt. The army could not have been more accommodating and helpful. It was late afternoon of a very dreary day when I was escorted in convoy to the site, not, as expected, by soldiers but by a lovely local man they employed for such duties. Aptly named Ray Parish, he had a touchingly deep love for his county and this church, and without him I might still be there, since as darkness crept in after photographing the church my truck got stuck in mud and only his expertise managed to extricate it. What a stunning place! The church could never have been near to its village, which was totally evacuated to form the training area during the Second World War and obviously very remote now, but it can never have been a very busy place. After what seemed like miles of winding track we stumbled upon this Norman round tower church standing alone, the sound of distant machine gun and canon fire making an already surreal experience even more so.

Although Stanford is a Saxon name this is most definitely a Norman church. The original round tower has an elegant octagonal top of a later date that evidently once had a conical cap, now gone, hopefully not as the result of a stray shell. Surrounding the octagon are four bell windows and four more blank windows, all with excellent fourteenth-century tracery and to the west of the tower, about two thirds of the way up, a single clock face. The rest of the building consists of nave, chancel and north and south aisles, all under an attractive red roof; now redundant it is well kept and in remarkably good condition. The churchyard, although now covered with long, deep grass, is spacious, although, thinking of it in the remote peace and quiet it must once have known, those resting there can hardly have expected that their final peace would be disturbed by the noise of war.

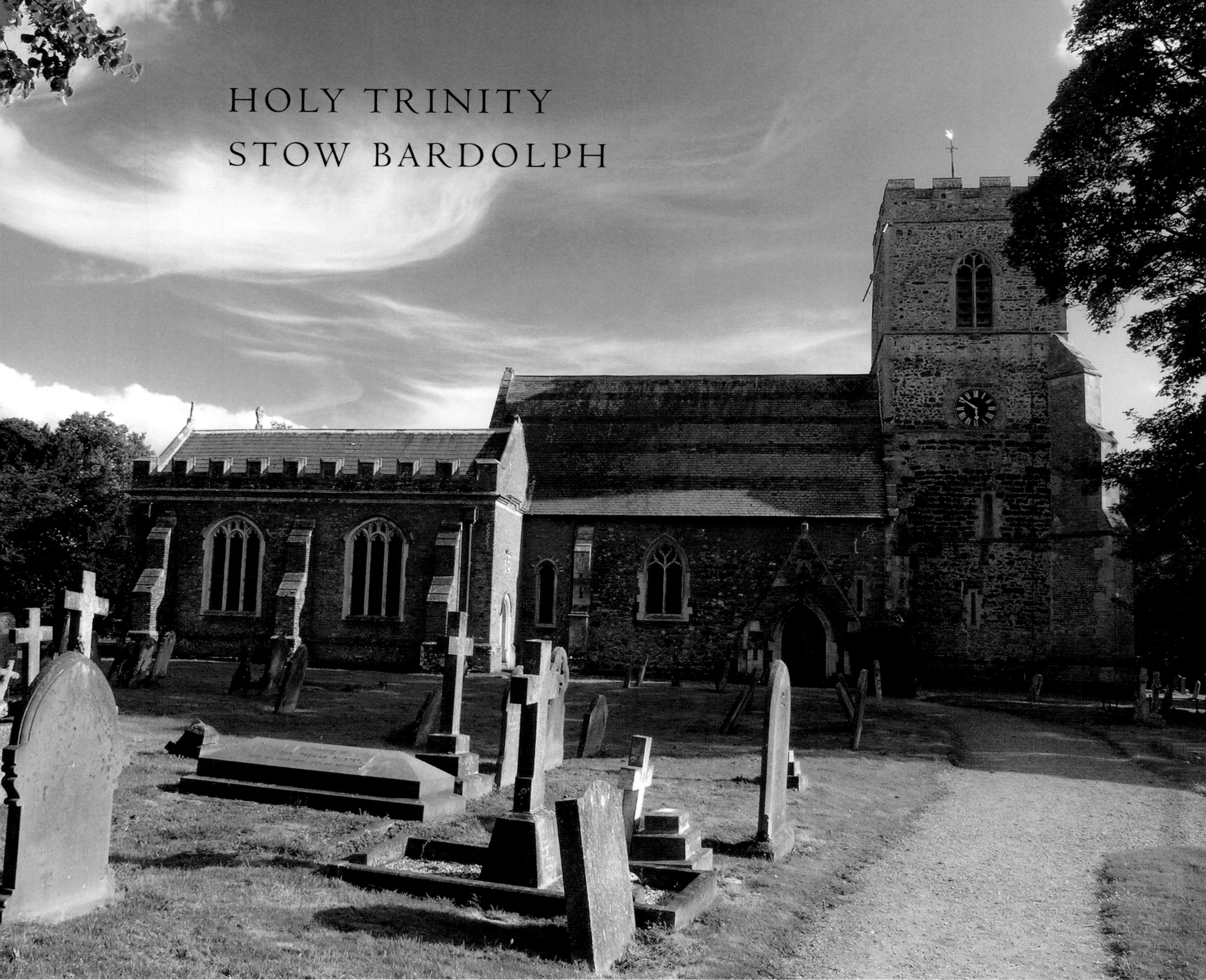

HOLY TRINITY STOW BARDOLPH

The original Norman church was replaced between 1189 and 1272 and was the subject of various adjustments and additions right up until the Victorians practically rebuilt the whole thing again in 1850. Apart from noting that the tower with its hefty brick buttresses still stands on its original Norman base there is little more to be said about the unprepossessing, but not unpleasing, exterior of this church because nothing about it could possibly compete with the unique oddness of its contents.

The Hare family, who first arrived at Stow Hall in 1553, dominate the history here and in 1624 John Hare built a brick mausoleum on

the north side of the chancel as 'a spacious dormitory for the internment of myself and my family'. It contains a number of impressive monuments to various members of that family. Firstly a wall tablet framed in alabaster with marbled columns surmounted with a coat of arms remembers Nicholas (d.1597). Then Sir Ralph Hare (d.1623), who built the village almshouses in 1603, is commemorated with a fine corniced tomb chest complete with Corinthian columns in gilded and painted alabaster. On the north wall is the imposing carved figure of Sir Thomas (d.1693) reclining in wig and Roman armour (the only example in Norfolk of a funereal fashion that only lasted for a very short period). Poor Sir Thomas died aged just thirty-six and this memorial was erected to 'the treasure of her heart and pleasure of her eye' by his wife Elizabeth, who did not rest beside him for a further fifty-six years. Another massive monument depicts Susanne

The monument to Sir Ralph Hare

The monument to Susanne Hare

The waxwork of Sarah Hare

(d.1741), seated and wearing billowing drapery. This is by Peter Scheemaker, famous for his statue of Shakespeare in Westminster Abbey, this being the only example of his work in Norfolk. There are other family members commemorated in this mausoleum, which is so unusually bright and airy that it is used to the present day as a Sunday school. One wonders if the children are ever allowed to view the scary contents of a mahogany cupboard in the corner. Hopefully not, since it contains yet another family memorial, by far the most gruesome. Sarah (d.1744) was the daughter of Sir Thomas and Elizabeth and her will was very specific about her funeral arrangements. It stated that she was to be 'buried by six poor people of the parish each to be paid 5 shillings for the trouble' and 'I desire to have my hands and face modelled in wax and put in a case with glass'. Before leaving, open the cupboard slowly and you will lessen the shock of being confronted by an extremely unattractive woman glaring smugly out at you. The work was conserved by Madame Tussauds in 1984 and is the only funerary waxwork to survive outside Westminster Abbey. A local story tells that she died of blood poisoning having pricked her finger while sewing aged just eighteen. Were it true she would have to have been one of the ugliest eighteen-year-olds of her day, but this is just a story. She was in fact fifty-one when she died – a little vain perhaps and certainly no sleeping beauty.

ST MARGARET STRATTON STRAWLESS

The monument to Henry Marsham

The monument to Thomas Marsham

I have visited hundreds of churches in the course of writing this series of books and to date I have never come across anything approaching the of warmth of welcome and pure kindness this church offers to all who enter it. Was this just a freak day or the remains of some other festivity? It felt as though this was how visitors are greeted every day of every year. Admittedly this was a gloriously sunny day in early May and the church and surrounding countryside sparkled, making all seem well with the world. What I encountered here was the work of people who understood the need for churches to invite people in. Those responsible cared deeply about their lovely church and wanted to share that love with all who came. On entering thorough a wide open door one is invited by a few small notices to a large table set to one side on which there are soft drinks and tea-making facilities and a delightful array of home made cakes and biscuits, to which one is encouraged to refresh oneself before enjoying the treasures the church has to offer. With a background such as mine I am experienced in marketing practices but here they are used with a subtlety that would put many major advertising agencies to shame. No mention is made of donations or paying for the refreshments left for the tired and grateful visitor, which of course ensures that all but the most churlish will be generous as they leave. A joy of an introduction to a joy of a church, and the cake was delicious.

Set in a pretty, well cared for churchyard, the broad, squat fifteenth-century west tower immediately catches the eye. Instead of pinnacles, it is topped by an interesting arrangement of figures, possibly representing the Evangelists, the whole supported by mighty diagonal buttresses. In 1422 money was left for the building of a tower, which it is generally agreed was meant to be much higher, but somehow never got beyond its present height. The earliest part of the building is a Norman doorway to the chancel, but this is now concealed by a slightly out-of-place brick vestry. Entry is through an old oak door leading into a most unusual foyer, with other doors leading off in every direction, an arrangement that the church leaflet caringly states 'prevents cold draughts in the worship area'. The interior is light but with a very unusual configuration that owes much to the fact that in the seventeenth century the brick south aisle was rebuilt to accommodate the impressive Marsham family tombs. For some reason this new aisle was divided from the nave by a metal screen composed of a series of arches, decorated at the bottom with an intermittent row of what appear to be large porcelain eggs and, although not ugly, it somewhat restricts that view of the monuments. Viewed from within the aisle, however, these stone monuments are impressive. At the east end, a reclining Thomas Marsham (d.1638) in his shroud attempts to rise from a black sarcophagus in answer to the clarion call sounded by an angel above him. Set in a grill below a remarkably fine but explicit representation of a charnel house full of hands, bones and skulls flanked by gravedigger's tools makes this the earliest Norfolk monument based on the theme of resurrection. On an adjacent wall another stone monument shows Henry Marsham (d.1692) alongside his twelve-year-old son and wife Anne, who both died in 1678, and an upright baby Margaret in swaddling. These truncated figures kneel, awkwardly, giving them in Mortlock's words 'the look of a family of amputees'. In the north-east corner of the nave there is also an effigy, 'the black abbess', thought to date from about 1300. Painted black she holds her heart in one hand. The windows have some fragments of fifteenth-century glass and hanging in the nave is a wonderful twenty-five-branch chandelier, said to have come from Russia in the seventeenth or eighteenth century but no one knows how or why. Nonetheless, it is really the peace and warmheartedness of this church that make it hard to leave or forget.

Detail of the monument to Thomas Marsham

ALL SAINTS TATTERSETT

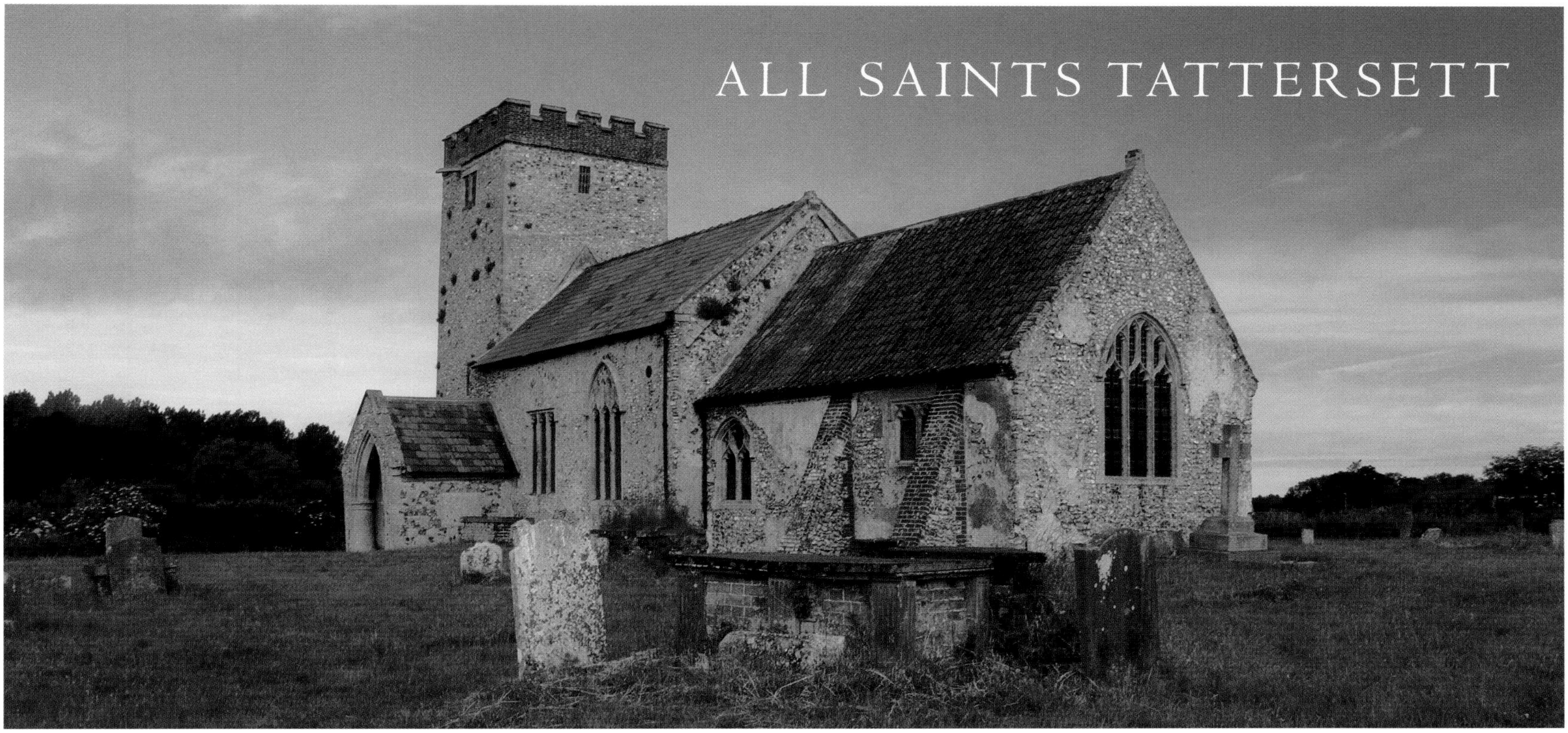

An alternative title for this book might be Hard to Find Norfolk Churches, and perhaps I have taken a perverse delight in seeking them out. This one is certainly highly qualified on that front. After journeying up and down lanes, sighting the tower then losing it again, eventually taking an uncertain ride down a grass-covered track for half a mile with the distinct possibility of being stranded, there it is – nowhere near a village. It stands high above the valley of the River Tat in a large churchyard and, from its well cared for state, it is obviously much loved by a congregation that, knowing its precise location, travels to it on a regular basis.

Essentially a thirteenth-century building with traces of an earlier Norman pedigree, it has two reinforcing red brick buttresses on the south of the chancel, a square tower with bell openings, and battlements also in red brick. The lavish use of red brick continues in the charming interior where it lines the sedilia and piscina, and although this is a far older building it is clear that a great deal of what we see today was added or restored in Tudor times.

Mortlock's acclaims 'the quiet triumph of its survival', a thought that is punctuated in the churchyard, where a recent and moving, albeit slightly peculiar, home made plaster headstone commemorating Ralph Elvis Mallet – obviously a local character with a musical inclination – triumphantly shares a place alongside ancient, grander and more traditional monuments. Its very existence is testimony to a caring and understanding community that will continue to guarantee the survival of this lovely and thought-provoking church.

The grave of Ralph Ellis Mallet

ST CLEMENT TERRINGTON ST CLEMENT

This massive structure is justifiably known by many as the 'Cathedral of the Marshes'.

Local legend has it that the tower looked so good while being constructed that the Devil tried to steal it but caught his foot on the church roof and dropped it. Less romantic but more likely is that the originally intention was to erect the tower on top of the choir between the nave and the chancel. This being marshland, the building was already subsiding and massive buttresses had been added, so the great weight of a tower would probably have caused the entire building to collapse. So it was built detached but barely eight feet from the western facade of the church. Vindication of the wisdom of this architectural decision came in the seventeenth century when the Wash (now miles away) broke down the sea wall, flooding the entire area and the local population only saved themselves by taking refuge in the tower, which stood firm against the devastation of their town.

Although there are traces of Norman, possibly even Saxon, origins it is, in the main, a thirteenth- and fourteenth-century building. The vast clerestory constitutes a veritable wall of glass, boasting fourteen three-light windows per side and, as if that were not enough, the chancel had its own clerestory added in Tudor times. The porch has a quatrefoil base course which matches that of the tower and once inside there is much to admire. A plain screen dating from 1788 divides the west end of the nave from the rest of the church and on the walls hang Decalogue prayer boards dating from 1635 that are reputedly among the finest in existence. Also on the walls are hatchments and a Royal Arms of Queen Anne painted on canvas, plus several interesting cartouche memorials. The great east window is an elaborate memorial to the local men who fell in the First World War, in all one hundred souls, an exceptionally high number from a small place and many families must have grieved multiple losses.

The fifteenth-century octagonal font has an impressive and extraordinary sixteenth-century cover, which opens up in sections to reveal a panoramic painting, probably Flemish, depicting the baptism, fasting and temptation of Christ with the Devil shown wearing a red cloak. Next to the door are two statues that were discovered hidden in the buttresses in 1887; one is of St Clement, the other St Christopher with Christ upon his shoulders. They were probably hidden there to avoid defacement during the Civil War and then simply forgotten. Although damaged they are very interesting examples of the legions of figures that once filled the now empty niches of so many churches.

The font

The porch

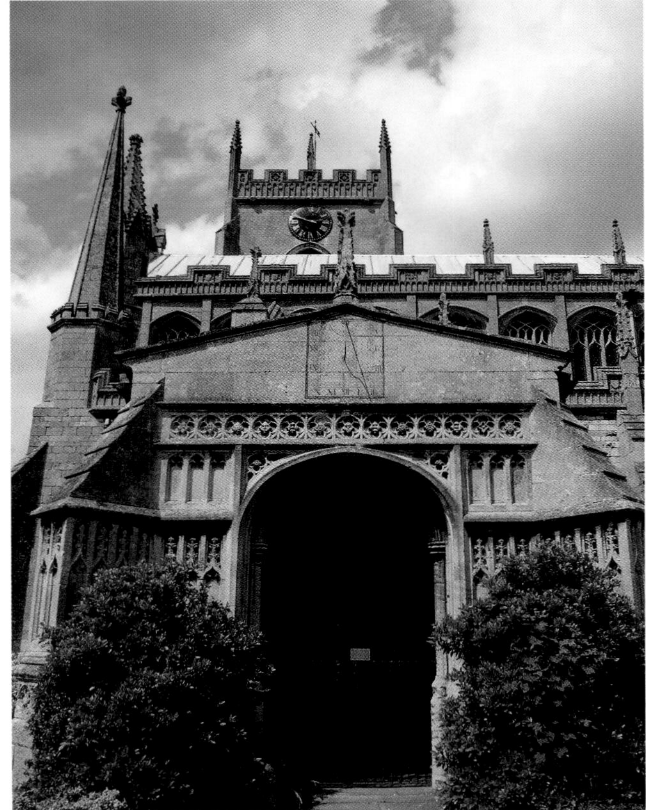

The monument to Dorothy Edwards and her husband

THE COLLEGIATE CHURCH OF ST MARTIN THOMPSON

The nave

The stalls

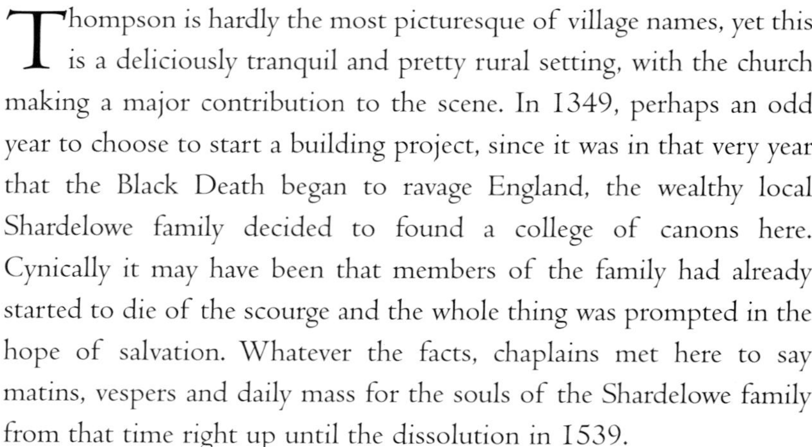

Thompson is hardly the most picturesque of village names, yet this is a deliciously tranquil and pretty rural setting, with the church making a major contribution to the scene. In 1349, perhaps an odd year to choose to start a building project, since it was in that very year that the Black Death began to ravage England, the wealthy local Shardelowe family decided to found a college of canons here. Cynically it may have been that members of the family had already started to die of the scourge and the whole thing was prompted in the hope of salvation. Whatever the facts, chaplains met here to say matins, vespers and daily mass for the souls of the Shardelowe family from that time right up until the dissolution in 1539.

The building, with its particularly lovely west window, is mostly fourteenth century, a south chapel being added in the fifteenth century by Sir Thomas de Shardelowe. Under a roof that was lowered to the present scissor-braced structure in 1608, the interior maintains the tranquillity of the exterior setting. At the west end of the nave are the Royal Arms of Queen Anne, dated 1705, and on the north side a Jacobean family pew stands opposite an odd-looking double-decker pulpit. Leading into the chancel is an elaborately carved early fourteenth-century screen which retains some colouring on its tracery of circles, ogee arches and, unusually, thin shafts painted in the manner of barbers' poles. The stalls of the collegiate fellows have seen much remedial work over the centuries, but four of them retain their misericords carved with heads and the Sharelowe arms. Both piscina and sedilia are in the Decorated style, the latter having little men peeping out from under the ogee arches. It is generally agreed that the dates 1625 and 1632 carved on two pews refer only to the carving of decorative thistles rather than the whole and the only point of contention comes from Pevsner, who feels that the claim that the organ case is by Pugin is 'unlikely'.

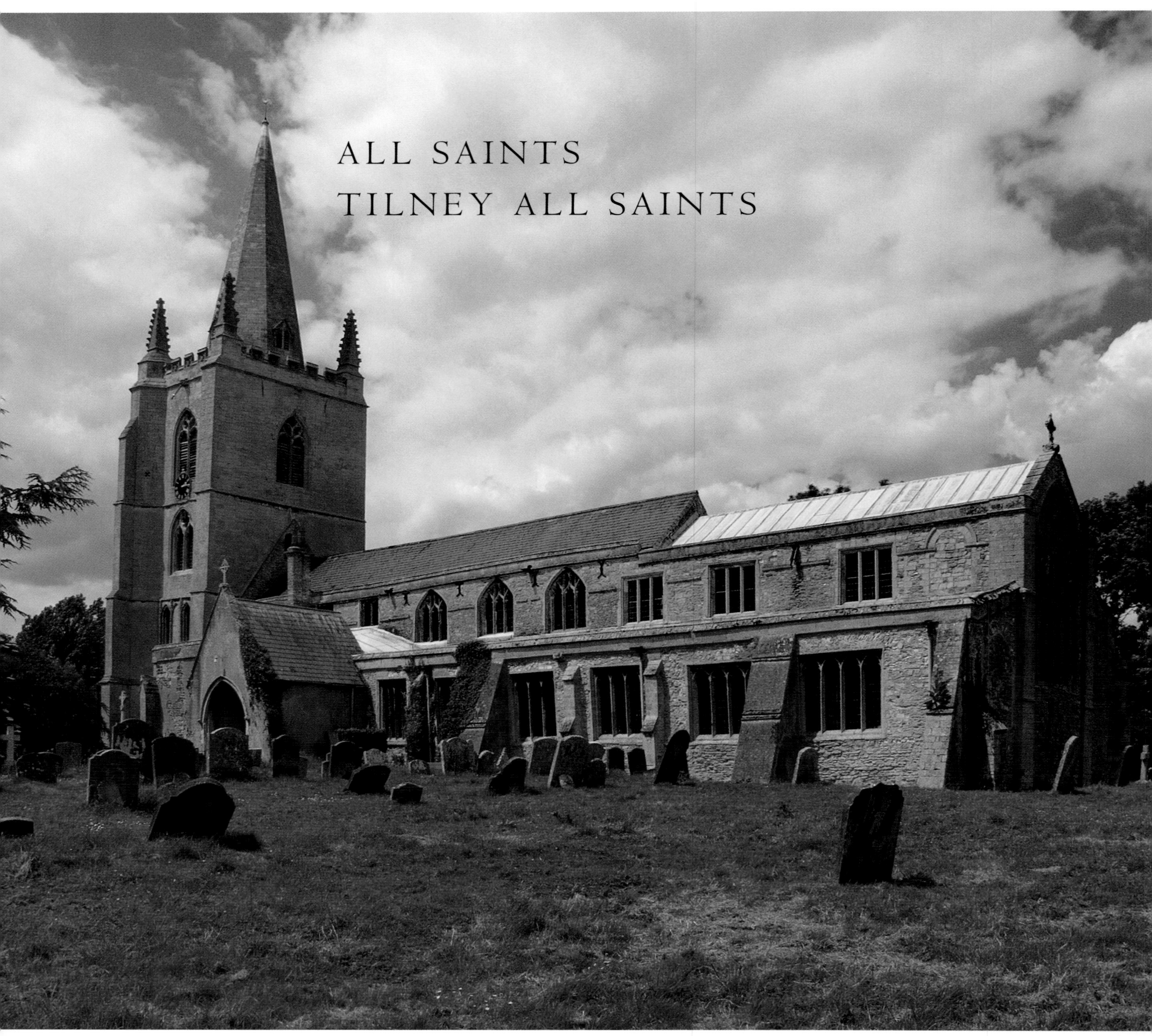

ALL SAINTS TILNEY ALL SAINTS

Built in the distinctive stone known as 'Barnack Rag', brought here from Northamtonshire quarries owned by the Abbey of Peterborough, this large church is an imposing sight, with its hefty tower. This is largely thirteenth-century but crowned by a handsome fourteenth-century upper story complete with ornamented pinnacles and a near perfect recessed spire. Unusually massive buttresses at the western corners of the tower make it appear far larger and are of special interest. The one to the north-west contains a small chamber with a vaulted ceiling and another chamber above it, approached by a staircase contained in the south-west buttress and linked through a narrow passage passing across the west window. The arcades can be accurately dated to around 1180 so a church certainly existed here in the twelfth century and possibly much earlier, although massive rebuilding work in the fifteenth century not only replaced the original clerestory but accounts for a great deal of the present building.

Inside a lovely double hammerbeam roof looms high above. Alternate rows of figures and heraldry decorate the lower hammers, the upper hammers being decorated with winged angels, but on closer inspection these turn out to be false hammers carrying no load, so this is, in fact, not a true double hammerbeam roof. Both Jacobean, the font and screen date from 1618 but the paraclose screens in the north and south aisles are fifteenth century, as are the piscina and sedilia. Close to the font is a grave slab bearing the cross pattée of the Knights Templar. This is possibly the grave of Baron Fredrick de Tylney, famous for his strength and size. He was knighted by Richard the Lionheart while on crusade and died at the Siege of Acre in 1291, his body being embalmed and brought back to this church. There is also a rare coat of arms of Queen Anne dated 1711, rare since she only reigned for twelve years and therefore there are very few in existence.

It is said that that the giant John Hickathrift, subject of many local stories, is buried in the churchyard, which contains a number of seventeenth- and eighteenth-century headstones and a memorial for John Eaton (d.1718), which reads:

The world's a City, full of crooked streets:
Death is the market place, where all men meet,
If life were merchandise, that men could buy,
Rich men would always live and poor men die.

The hammerbeam roof

Misericord

ST PETER AND ST PAUL TUTTINGTON

As usual, some argue that this round tower, with its later, somewhat unusual spike, is Norman while some claim it as Saxon. This is often a contentious point and in this case the jury must probably remain out. However, what can be said with certainty is that the tower is oldest part of the church, since the rest was almost completely rebuilt in 1450. The disproportionately tall, narrow south porch once had two storeys but, for reasons unknown, the upper floor was removed at some time in the past.

Inside is a pulpit dated 1635, with a quaint hourglass stand and, shortly after that date, in 1638, the fifteenth-century octagonal font acquired its attractive cover. However, it is the carvings on the benches that capture the eye; they present a carnival of morality tale and legend using quaintly rural imagery. Animals leap and humans, some playing instruments, cavort, among them an extraordinary Elephant and Castle, which to my mind surely refers to Catherine of Aragon's procession to London to meet and marry her brother-in-law Henry VIII.

ST ANDREW
WALPOLE ST ANDREW

There can't be many places where two such impressive, yet completely different churches stand just a meadow or two apart, but such is the case in the Walpoles. The big marshland church of St Andrew, distinct in its redbrick hue, was built to replace a much earlier church between 1420 and 1470. The Perpendicular west tower, with its stair rising to an octagonal turret, has, within its south-west buttress, a room thought by some to have been an anchorite cell. Others claim it as a shrine for those about to make the extremely hazardous trip across the treacherous Wash to Lincolnshire. What makes the latter theory more plausible is the fact that it was in this parish that King John lost his crown jewels while, against all local advice, he attempted to cross the Wash to Long Sutton in 1216.

As a complement to its striking exterior the lofty interior of this church is lit by an eight-windowed clerestory and boasts particularly tall arcades and an admirable fifteenth-century font that stands on a much earlier perpendicular base. Behind the fine seventeenth-century pulpit, which still retains its hourglass bracket, is a painting which was once the original alter piece. This is the work of Sebastino Ricci and it is the only example of his work in an English church.

ST PETER
WALPOLE ST PETER

This other Walpole church was built with money made from sheep. Deservedly known as the 'Queen of the Marshland', the tower, built around 1300, is the oldest part and all that survived a devastating flood in 1337. As if that were not enough this was followed by the plague in 1348 and it was a decade before building work resumed. The nave and chancel were all one until the present chancel was added in 1420, the splendid porch following about 1430.

A very unusual feature of the exterior of this fascinating building is that the chancel extends to the edge of the churchyard where a passageway passes under the sanctuary. Known as the 'bolt hole', practically a small street under a marvellous vaulted roof, it was probably used for processions which could circle the church without those taking part ever having to leave consecrated ground.

The gorgeous south porch leads through an original oak door to an interior that does justice to such an inspired exterior. There is a marvellous collection of carved benches and the faded remains of a doom painting fill the chancel arch, beneath which is the base of a once lovely rood screen crudely painted with saints. At the west end of the nave a seventeenth-century screen runs across the entire building and the base of the font commands 'Thynk and Thank 1582'. The peculiar sentry box next to the tower arch turns out to have been, up until the ninteenth century, a portable shelter for the priest when conducting graveside services in inclement weather.

ALL SAINTS WATERDEN

The nave and chancel

There is no longer a village, so one could drive up and down constantly passing this church without ever noticing it, tucked unassumingly down a long winding track through what appears to be just a gap in a hedge. Indeed it was only after stopping a strolling stranger who informed me that his son was mowing the grass there at that very moment that I finally located it. This alone made it clear that from ruin and disuse this church was now much loved and had been brought back to life by caring locals. There is nothing here of outstanding interest except ancient rural history. All we know about the tower is that it collapsed at some time, and now there is only a primitive wooden bell tower. The north and south doors are Norman, possibly Saxon, but under the eaves to the north there are blocked windows that are definitely Saxon. A small porch with Early English quatrefoil windows leads to an interior of which the only comment that comes to mind is, once again, great age and a simple feeling of kindness.

Was the visit worthwhile? Yes, because to miss these ancient, often hidden, gems is to forego an opportunity of tasting what it might have been like to have lived and worshipped in these remote locations and to marvel that through the centuries of good and bad times these little churches have had the habit of resurrecting themselves just when it seemed all was lost.

ST MARY WEETING

Nothing is what it seems here. Seen from a particular angle and in the conditions in which it is shown here, it appears to be in a wild, remote and romantic spot, but in fact it is practically on top of an ever-expanding urban housing estate. A Norman round tower? Well yes and no. It was, but the original tower was completely replaced in 1868. That said it was done beautifully and this is a lovely little church.

Standing in a large open churchyard the nave has a very steep pitch and big Perpendicular windows with embattled transoms. Decorative in style, the chancel has a superb five-light east window, its reticulated tracery pierced at the top by an octofoil circle, which on the inside has statue niches on both sides.

Heavy Victorian restoration both inside and out has been generally sympathetic and the surprisingly spacious interior is neat and trim. There is a small but functional four-bay arcade dating from the fourteenth century and in the sanctuary a rare pair of thirteenth-century quatrefoil piscina bowls, which have been cut out of the actual windowsill. In some ways this is almost a reproduction of a church that once was but it has been done with much care, and hopefully what we see now may now go on to serve its congregation for another thousand years.

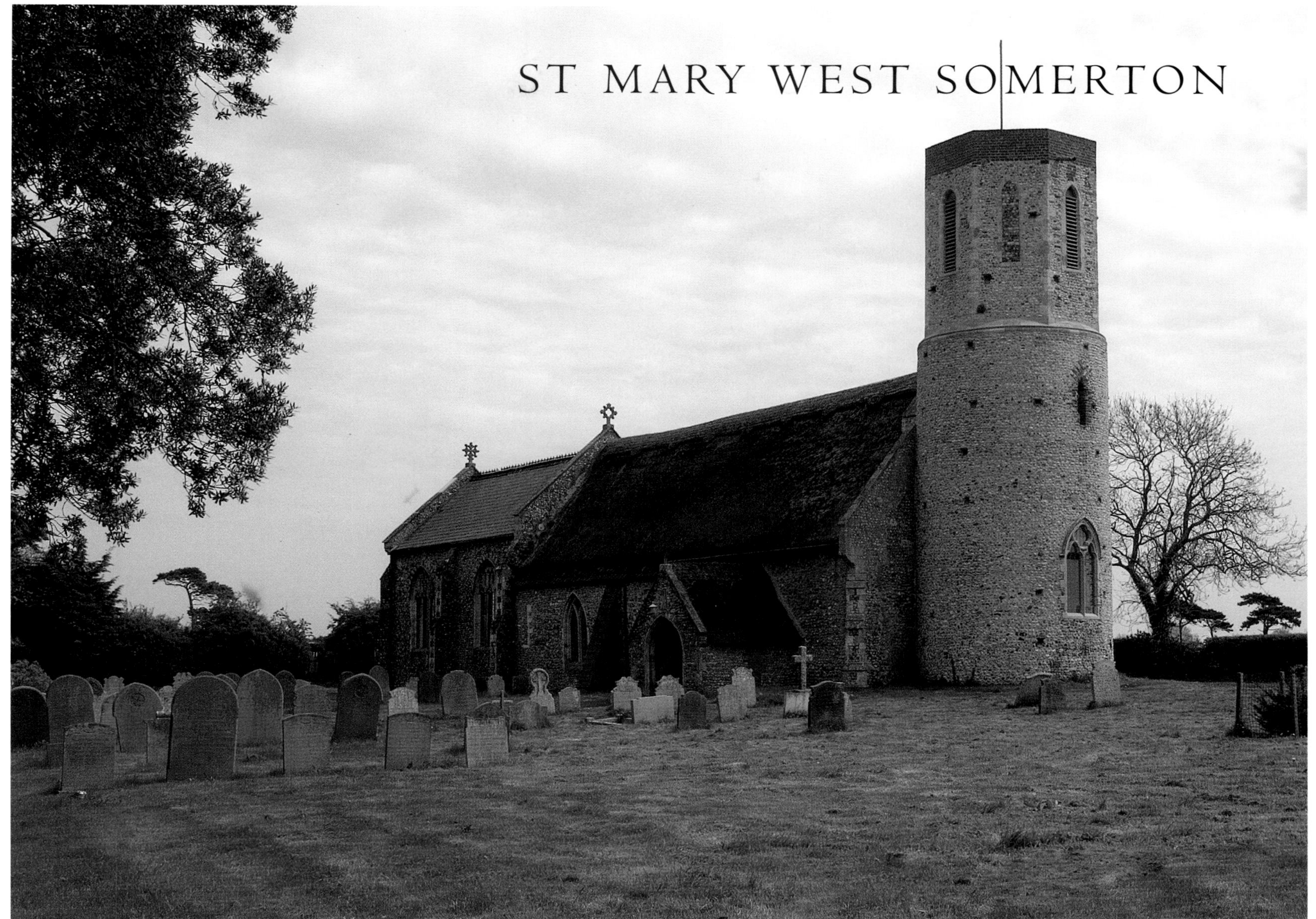

ST MARY WEST SOMERTON

From an enviable setting this lovely church stares across the marshes towards the sea. A list of its pedigree is suffice to proclaim its religious and historic significance over a span of a thousand years. A flint round tower, which is very probably Saxon, crowned with a sixteenth-century brick parapet, an eleventh-century thatched nave with the remnants of fourteenth-century wall paintings, a fifteenth-century chancel, porch and screen, plus a Decalogue board dated 1560. What more could one ask? The grave of a giant in the churchyard? Well yes, for Robert Hales the 'Norfolk Giant' who stood seven foot eight inches in his stocking feet, toured the world in sideshows and was introduced to Queen Victoria and eventually became the local inn keeper is buried here.

ST MARY
WEST WALTON

West Walton is pretty much as far west as you can go in Norfolk; a hop and a skip and you are in Cambridgeshire. The design of this church owes far more, however, to the style of Lincolnshire parish churches. This is marshland and that is the reason why the massive bell tower stands separate from the church, which was built during the period 1225–40, and followed a little later. The builders realised the massive tower planned would not stand on the same marshy ground as the church, for they had noticed that there were a number of underground springs beneath it. So they decided to position the tower on the firmest land in the parish, which happened to be just south of the church, and hence the separation.

The top of the tower favours the Perpendicular style, but the dogtooth decoration of the lower arches is Early Gothic, placing its origin to around 1250 and, although now redundant and no longer sturdy enough for the ringing of bells, it is beautifully maintained by the Churches Conservation Trust. If seen as a gateway to the church the function of the tower makes sense of the initially peculiar layout, and viewed from under its arches the church takes its rightful place an overall design plan. The porch is truly sumptuous, but was much deeper and even grander before it suffered severe truncation in the fourteenth century when the aisles were widened. The interior is no less impressive. In between the nave arches, under a hammerbeam roof held aloft by carved wooden angels that hold shields displaying the instruments of the Passion, are some very unusual eighteenth-century paintings representing the tribes of Israel, the most recognisable being the lion of Judah on the south side. Higher up on the clerestory walls there is much older decorative painting and the capital of every stone column is carved with its own, entirely individual and different leaf and foliage decoration. Unlike other churches that present numerous contributing factors to their overall story this church proclaims itself in a superb feat of medieval architectural genius.

The hammerbeam roof

The south arcade

Exterior from the south-east

ALL SAINTS WHEATACRE

Although a county of mainly flint churches there are other red brick churches in Norfolk, but nothing to remotely compare with this. Even Essex, with its preponderance of striking red brick has nothing quite like it. Sheer genius lies behind the choice of the huge chequerwork pattern of red brick and dressed flint used on the tower, and it is not only conceived but executed with fantastic panache. It covers the massively buttressed early-sixteenth-century tower, blended into a battlemented final stage and absorbing bell openings that are possibly seventeenth century. The whole thing seems to vibrate in the sunlight. The west doorway has a multi-stepped brick arch, while the fourteenth-century south doorway has a lovely ogee hood mould with nicely carved heads, one male, one female, acting as stops.

The nave was rebuilt about the same time as the tower, but sadly most of the rest is rather heavy-handed Victorian restoration and the interior suffers most of the over-zealous attentions of the Victorians. The font, however, tucked away in the south-west corner, seems to have slipped past them and although pretty traditional, with lions, shields and flowers, it has details picked out in colour, some possibly original. On a counterweight above it a somewhat peculiar cover, vaguely in the Arts and Crafts style, has rather flatly carved fruit and flowers. Between the chancel and north chapel there is a screen dated 1904, which, although more restrained, appears to be by the same hand as the font cover.

ST MARY MAGDALEN WIGGENHALL

If you look to the bottom right of the photograph you will see a peacock wandering contentedly around the churchyard, as locals informed me it often does. I was unable to get a shot of it in full display in front of the church but it did spread its beautiful feathered fan once, but far from upstaging the church it merely endorsed the fact that this church, externally and internally, is also about colour. It is a peacock of a church.

As is so often the case, the tower is the oldest part of this church; most of the rest is fifteenth century. It is the blended carr and freestone of the tower, mixed with red brick elsewhere that makes the exterior so sumptuously colourful. At the eastern end of the nave, two large pinnacled turrets housing rood staircases neatly balance the building. A lovely red brick south porch once had an upper floor for accommodating visiting priests and doubled as a village school, but it has long gone. In 1432 one Philip Mayner left 5 marks (£3-6-8d, or about £1000 nowadays) towards rebuilding costs. However, the two main benefactors of this building were the Ingoldsthorps and the powerful Howard families, whose arms can be seen in the spandrels above the internal doorway of the porch.

Once inside the colour experience continues as light floods in from both the clerestory and the arcades. At the west end of the north aisle are four panels from the original rood, each painted with one of the Evangelists, while at the east end are parts of the fifteenth-century paraclose screens that originally enclosed chapels. But the north aisle is where the treasure lies. Here sunlight flickers and weaves through some remarkable, stained glass, thought to have been donated in 1450 by Isabel Ingoldisthorp, wife of Lord Monacute. The tracery lights of the windows are filled with no less than forty little figures representing an extraordinarily obscure group of saints, bishops and popes, many of whom are individually named, such St Callistus, St Hippolytus, St Prosdecimus and St Desiderius. The reasons for the choice of such an unusually eclectic group of saints is not clear, but in view of the blatantly popish subject matter of the windows, it's a miracle they survived iconoclastic destruction. On that point, however, it was not bigoted fanatics from centuries ago that wrought destruction here; it was empty-headed do-gooders. There was once a marvellous doom painting, wantonly obliterated in 1900 by the church wardens, who whitewashed over it in the hope of pleasing a new parson about to take up office.

Stained glass

Stained glass

ST MARY AND ST THOMAS OF CANTERBURY WYMONDHAM

Wymondham is a very pretty market town, its parish church towering commandingly over it, an unusual and massive structure in a picture postcard setting. But size isn't everything, and therein lay the problem. In its early history the clergy had ideas that did not concur with those of the parishioners, and the relationship between them was for centuries fraught with argument, legal battle and, often, near riot.

Having gallantly supported William the Conqueror at Hastings, William d'Albini had, as a reward, lands granted to him, among which was Wymondham. D'Albini's brother was Abbot of the Benedictine establishment at St Albans and between them they decided to build not just a church in Wymondham but a dual-purpose complex for use both as a monastery and parish church. Building started in 1107 and the enormous edifice, 200 feet long with twin towers at the west end and a big central tower crossed by north and south trancepts plus cloisters and domestic buildings, was completed by 1130. Twelve monks immediately took up residence and the trouble began. From the outset the monks imagined they were in charge and took a very high-handed attitude towards the locals, but these were Norfolk locals and they were having none of it. So from the start clergy and parishioners did not get on at all. Dispute followed argument, culminating in the Pope being called on to mediate and eventually a shaky compromise was reached when the parishioners were granted exclusive use of the nave, north aisle and north-west tower, and the monks the rest. However, in the fourteenth-century the central tower was in poor condition and the monks pulled it down to build another one further west. In the interim they had installed their bells in the north-west tower (which belonged to the parish) and they now moved them back to their new tower and, without so much as a by your leave, blocked the entrance so the parishioners could not use their tower or bells. All hell broke loose and this time the Archbishop of Canterbury was called in. The parish was given permission to have their own bells and not rely on those belonging to and rung by the monks. Three thousand, eight hundred parishioners (which seems an enormous number for the fourteenth century) promptly signed a petition to build a new tower and a mere twenty years of further argument culminated in that tower being finished in 1448. After their triumph the townsfolk then rebuilt the north aisle and gave the nave a clerestory and at long last there was a shaky peace between monks and locals. Then came the Dissolution, which sealed the fate of the monastery with the last abbot, Elisha Ferrers, wisely proclaiming himself Vicar of Wymondham and letting the parishioners use parts of the dissolved monastery's building materials to build a new south aisle.

With all this going on one questions whether anyone had any time the glory of God. Apparently yes, for despite the endless argument and bickering that factions, committees and differing beliefs indulged in during the history of this church, we are left somewhat surprisingly with a building that is inspired. Despite the pettiness that contributed to its creation, it is a church that boasts not only an awesome exterior but a vast interior complete with a magical hammerbeam roof held aloft by a host of beautifully carved angels who never got involved in the arguments, plus a glorious rederos designed in 1919 by Sir Ninian Comper as a memorial to that unsurpassable example of man's unending folly, the Great War.

GLOSSARY

aisle The peripheral space usually running parallel with the nave; the chancel and transepts of a church may also be aisled.

alabaster A soft natural stone used for delicate carving. It is a granular form of gypsum, usually whitish-pink or yellowish in colour. It can be made nearly opaque by heating but the best is translucent white.

arcade A series of arches supported by pillars running down the sides of the nave of a church with aisles.

Arts and Crafts Movement A late nineteenth- to early twentieth-century movement opposing mass production and favouring hand crafted objects, taking its inspiration from the work of William Morris.

bay The area between two columns or piers of a row and including the wall and ceiling of the area, also applied to any area of wall surface divided by windows or a large vertical feature.

bellcote The framework on a roof from which the bells are hung.

bench ends The vertical section of the benches adjacent to an aisle, often richly carved with depictions of people, biblical scenes, grotesques and animals from nature or mythology.

box pews Large pews panelled to waist height or more, often with cushioned seats on three sides and sometimes even curtains. They are entered by a door from the aisle. Nicknamed box pews for their resemblance to horse boxes, they became popular in the seventeenth and early eighteenth century but in the restorations of the nineteenth century many disappeared.

brass An incised memorial made in an alloy called latten, bearing a portrait or inscription and usually found on the floor or on the top of tombs. The earliest brass in England is said to be dated 1277 (Sir John d'Abernon at Stoke Abernon in Surrey). Brasses were common until the first half of the seventeenth century, although there are some modern examples. The practice of taking rubbings has become very popular.

buttress A brickwork or masonry support projecting from (flying buttress) or built against a wall to give additional support.

capital The usually decorated and ornamented top of a column or pillar, from which the supported arch springs.

chancel The part of a church, including the altar and choir, reserved for the clergy. Sometimes separated from the nave by a rood screen.

cinquefoil see trefoil

clerestory An upper storey standing clear of its adjacent roofs and pierced by windows, the number of which usually corresponds to the number of bays in the arcade below.

corbel A block of stone projecting from a wall, supporting some horizontal feature. Often carved or moulded.

crocketed Small projecting sculptural feature in the form of leaves or flowers, used on pinnacles, spires, canopies, etc., first appearing in the Decorated period in the first half of fourteenth century, carried through to the later Perpendicular style.

cupola Small polygonal or circular domed turret crowning a roof.

Decorated Style of English Gothic architecture covering the period from 1290 to 1350.

diaper A repeating decorative pattern executed in low relief carving or painted on a play wall surface, often square or diamond shaped in design.

doom painting A depiction of the Last Judgment, normally found painted over the chancel arch (which symbolically separated earthly from heavenly things). Christ is typically represented sitting on a rainbow with souls being weighed below before being sent to join the blessed on his right hand side or the damned on his left.

dormer window A window set vertically in a small gable projecting from a sloping roof.

fleurons Decorative carved flowers or leaves.

flushwork The decorative use of flint in conjunction with dressed stone to form patterns, tracery and sometimes lettering and initials.

font A structure designed to hold the holy water that is used at baptism. Most are made of stone but a few lead ones survive.

gothic Period of architecture from the twelfth to the fifteenth century and embodied in the Early English and Decorated styles. The original influence was the architecture of twelfth-century France.

hammerbeam Projecting right-angled beam or bracket, shaped like a hammer at the foot of the curved member or principal rafter in a wooden roof. Often decorated and supporting vertical or arched braces.

hatchment Diamond-shaped memorial painting depicting the arms or family crest of the deceased against a background that shows their sex and marital status. These boards were carried in procession at the burial of the holder of the arms. For some months after they were kept at the deceased's house then finally transferred to the church walls.

lancet Tall narrow light which is sharply pointed at the top and a feature of early English architecture. Often found in groups of three and five, groups of seven are known but far less common.

linenfold Series of wooden panels, carved to look like pieces of material hanging vertically in natural folds.

misericord A carved bracket supporting a hinged seat when it is turned up for use. Often beautifully carved and ornamented with both ecclesiastical subjects as well as more grotesque and eccentric themes.

nave The area between the chancel and the west end, in which the congregation is housed during services.

niche Vertical hollow or ornamental recess in a wall, designed to hold a small statue.

Norman English building style from 1066–1200. Impressive massive buildings with a large variety of mouldings on arches and doorways, semi-circular arches, barrel vaults and mostly square towers. Aisles were a later addition of the period.

octofoil see trefoil

ogee A continuous flowing S-shaped arch or moulding. A convex curve flows into a concave one. They are not usually very large since the design is not capable of bearing heavy loads, but their elegance adorns the heads of canopies over piscina, sedilia and other delicate traceries.

paraclose screen The partition or screen around a shrine, chapel or tomb, in order to separate it from the main body of the church.

pedestal Supporting base between a column and the plinth.

Perpendicular Style running from about 1350–1539, a period when church building achieved its ultimate splendour with lofty proportions, vertical lines, huge windows, high arches, traceried panels and elaborate decoration, battlemented parapets and flying buttresses. Much of this was made possible by the wealth of wool merchants.

pews Wooden bench seats often enclosed by high walls with doors.

piscina Niche containing a stone bowl or drain. Usually built into a wall of the chancel near an altar. Sometimes built under an elaborate canopy. Used for washing sacred vessels the water drained to consecrated ground outside the church walls.

poppyhead A floral or leaf-like carving decorating a bench or choir stall.

pulpit Raised platform from which the preacher delivers his sermon. Most are carved in wood but there are a few rare stone ones.

quatrefoil see trefoil

reredos Decorated screen or wall-covering behind an altar beneath the east window. Can be tapestry, painting or a stone construction shaped to show the twelve apostles.

rood beam Horizontal beam spanning the chancel and sometimes the aisles supports a representation of a crucifix (rood).

rood screen A wooden or stone screen dividing the nave from choir and chancel, often elaborately carved and painted.

sanctuary Area to the east of the altar rails all around and including the altar.

Saxon Period covering roughly 600–1066. The churches built at this time were simple, single or two-cell buildings with a western entrance often in wood but later in stone. Many round towers are of Saxon origin with later churches added.

scissor-beam A roof in which the beams are crossed and interlocked diagonally in the shape of an open pair of scissors.

sedilia Set of three or four seats, recessed in niches in the south wall of the chancel, used by the priest and his assistants. Often set under decorative canopied arches.

spandrel The space between two arches, also the triangle-shaped blocking between the posts and beams of screens or roofs.

spire Tall conical structure tapering to a point, often topped with a weather vane, and built on top of a tower. Differs from a steeple in that it can be seen as a separate appendage to the tower; a steeple is an integral part of it.

table tomb Masonry tomb in the shape of an altar.

tower arch The arch leading from the nave into the interior of the tower.

tracery Ornamental work in wood or stone in a window screen or panelling.

transepts Arms projecting from the point where nave and chancel meet in a traditional cruciform church.

trefoil From the twelfth century, foils were a much used decoration in Gothic churches. The Early English style produced the trefoiled (three leafed shape), intended to represent the Trinity. This was followed by the quatrefoil (four leafed) the cinquefoil (five leafed) and the octofoil (eight leafed).

vault Arched roof, ceiling or arch-like structures with ribs radiating from one central point.